ADOLESCENCE INTERRUPTED

ADOLESCENCE INTERRUPTED

Blair Patrick Schuyler

Copyright © 2015 by Blair Patrick Schuyler

Book cover design and author photo by Eric Soboleski
(http://www.beforeinfinity.com)

Library of Congress Control Number: 2015901124
ISBN: 9781544875095

All rights reserved. No part of this book may be reproduced or transmitted in any form or by any means, electronic or mechanical, including photocopying, recording, or by any information storage and retrieval system, without permission in writing from the copyright owner.

Any people depicted in stock imagery provided by Thinkstock are models, and such images are being used for illustrative purposes only.
Certain stock imagery © Thinkstock.

TO MY FAMILY, FRIENDS, AND DOCTORS who consistently supplied the oxygen each time I slipped beneath the waterline.

TO KAREN, DIANE, MAUREEN, AND MARY. Your relentless stream of support made this book a reality.

TO MOM. Words can't begin to express my gratitude for your limitless love and immeasurable sacrifice. You not only gave me life, you enabled me to live it.

CONTENTS

The First Strike 9

The Guessing Game 16

The Realization 21

The Transformation 29

The Homecoming 35

The Warning Signs 39

The Roller Coaster Climb 42

The Unraveling 52

The Collapse 64

The Life Between 78

The Balance 91

The Lake Effect 100

The Boiling Point 112

The Plan 131

The Main Event 138

The Courage 148

THE FIRST STRIKE

THE POUNDING WAS relentless. Drumming palpitations started from the base of my skull, steadily built momentum, and crashed with conviction at the temples. It was cyclical, like waves smashing on a shore. But these tides came with little warning other than a stinging bite at my brain stem. The slightest tingle delivered a surge of fleeting paralysis. Each time the pins and needles arrived, I braced myself for impact.

The numbness served as a form of air traffic control. As soon as I felt my neck lock, pressure would build, and a mountain of pain was forced from the back of my head to the front of my eyes. This onslaught concluded with a brief moment of blackness. Then, as fragments of vision slowly returned, my body attempted to recover from the attack. Recuperation was hindered by fluctuations in the rhythm and severity of each swell. I was a surfer in a riptide, gasping for oxygen and watching the shrinking shore. But the mainframe's primary objective is to protect and survive, even when it's the orchestrator of the assault.

A headache and projectile vomiting accompanied the waves. In distress, the system will do anything in its power to sustain itself. Increased compression in the brain can be slightly alleviated by regurgitation. Although this did little to lessen the pain and dizziness, the cranial tension subsided for a while. However, each storm brought with it a fresh crop of pressure, nausea, and momentary blindness. Pain, confusion, trepidation, and shock. This was my world on an early January morning in eighth grade.

It was the first night of ski club. I couldn't have been more excited. I waited all winter recess for this. For eight Fridays, my best friends and potential young crushes would be given almost carte blanche to bend every behavioral rule in our attempts to breach the margins of human downhill speed limits.

We believed we could do anything under this guise of freedom. We were, of course, chaperoned, but the anonymity of a dark mountain coupled with the mentality of the indestructible teenager made for some pretty impressive feelings of liberation. Junior high is a hotbed of hormone activity, and putting a healthy mix of hyper happy teens on a few buses and sending them off to a nearly vacant ski mountain on a Friday night was as close to a picture of heaven pubescent boys would ever see.

This was my second year, so I knew exactly what to expect. Skis were sharpened and packed snugly in their bag. Boots, hats, gloves, hand warmers, and mix tapes were all accounted for and readily available. Comfortable school clothes that could double as slope-ready attire were essential because no one wanted to change after class or at the mountain for a number of reasons. First, the idea of thirteen-year-old boys undressing in front of anyone (especially girls) was enough to induce panic attacks. Second, time spent getting into another outfit was time lost on the lift. Third, when that bus finally pulled into the lodge, anticipation was in overdrive. We would have sat in our seats with boots and skis locked and loaded if possible. The night disappeared quickly enough. Extraneous delays were a definite foul.

The mix tape, specifically, was a crucial element to the nearly sixty-minute road trip. All tapes were played on mini-boom boxes, so proper song selections and clever track transitions spoke volumes about personality, ironic wit, and overall coolness. Most of these repetitive gems were captured from a popular nightly radio countdown, so the idea that any of us were practicing one shred of individuality is pretty laughable. But we proudly showcased our skills and sang along to our favorites, deliberately injecting faculty names into the choruses and inappropriate jokes into every verse. It was comic gold, and the laughter was loud.

The teachers and chaperones in the front of the bus would pretend to ignore the absurdly crude improvisations, but an overtly stern stare was directed to the backseats when our material got too scatological or sexual for ski trips. Of course, this did little to dissuade our fun and mostly served to heighten our amusement. At that age, there really is no line that can't be crossed. Forget the "terrible twos," thirteen- and fourteen-year-old boys are just about the wildest creatures in existence. Competition, cockiness, confusion, disillusion, awkwardness, and questionable fashion choices. This was our self-conscious luminescent canvas. We might have painted it with clumsy hands, but we painted it with pride.

We were good kids, but we knew how to push boundaries, basking in the glory of our own productions. Our class was pretty impressed with its particular brand of antics, and we were probably a little big for our teenage britches. But we came from solid homes, had good hearts, and simply found unique ways to amuse ourselves.

So with my bags and clothes laid out for the morning, I got into bed earlier than normal. It's never easy to get to sleep with excitement rattling through my body, so I did my best to block out the thoughts of the following day's adventures, and I closed my eyes.

The night was restless. I was unsettled, anxious, and cramped. I chalked it up to an overabundance of thoughts and tried to force myself back to sleep. The more I stressed about being awake, the longer I stayed that way. It felt like Christmas Eve or the night before an important presentation. I was a squirming, frazzled insomniac. It wasn't long before I just wanted the cycle to end so I could start my day. Little did I know a grave dawn was approaching.

Part of me wishes that I paid more attention to that night. If there were a way to box those memories and use them as momentary comforts for the roads that lay ahead, I would have savored that body, that frame. My hands would have held tightly to a skull that was smooth and round and whole. My eyes would have remembered the capacity for unrestricted peripheral vision. I would have stretched my neck without restraint and felt an abdomen free of scars, gashes, and synthetic implants. I would have taken mental photographs of a pristine hairline, and I would have soaked in the intoxicating sensation of physical health. I would have locked away the feeling of being unhampered by worry and that anything was possible. That night was a tangible time stamp of my innocence. It was, for fear of sounding melodramatic, the last time I would be normal.

The buzz of the alarm clock came as no surprise. I had been awake for half the night, so the obnoxious digital readout was nothing more than a nagging reminder. I got out of bed, frustrated and unjustifiably angry with myself. The whole point of getting to sleep early was to avoid this grogginess. My plan was ruined, and I felt awful. But the level of my disappointment was unreasonable. The lack of control over my senses and the pain pounding in my head left me without any measure to regulate emotions and thoughts. It was unnerving.

As I stumbled out of the bedroom, an overwhelming lack of balance and the sense that I was floating above the floor was too much to comprehend. My justification was the lack of rest, but I knew it was something more. This bizarre, chaotic earthquake was rocking my body and brain, and I actually thought I might have caught some strange twenty-four-hour bug. I rarely got sick, but this was much more than insomnia. So I figured I would simply push through the morning and hopefully feel better by the end of the day. Wishful thinking at its best.

When I stepped into the shower, things rapidly got worse. With the hot water running down my back, I swayed side-to-side, trying to find some semblance of stability. The headache grew considerably stronger, and the nausea intensified. I reached for the shampoo and saw tiny men rappelling from the top of the bottle to the base of the tile sill using miniature ropes. They assembled in a small pack and ran across the ledge. I watched them do this repeatedly. Oddly, I wasn't terrified or confused. It all seemed perfectly normal, and I was actually impressed by their rigorous attention to form and technique. It was like watching ants uniformly file into their hill. I was awed and intrigued. I can't even begin to estimate how long I stood there, watching the proceedings and letting the water hit my spine. But a violent bout of vomiting rocked me back to reality.

This would prove to be the start of a very reliable pattern: dizziness, head pressure, nausea, vomiting, and relief. I became increasingly familiar with these symptoms and the brief respite I got from the routine expulsion. It was a frightening (and later, disheartening) framework upon which my every move and decision in life would be based. There was no escape when that first inkling of dizziness began to materialize, and that glaring self-awareness was the most traumatic and heartbreaking aspect of the process.

My emotions were erratic, and I found myself standing in the shower, sobbing. I was upset, but at the same time, I was so completely unaware of why my body was reacting like that. I had never experienced that level of internal disruption. I was sick, but my gut said it was something more. The tears of frustration and anger flowed freely as I finally stepped out of the tub.

Mom heard the crying and came to the door. She was genuinely concerned. I attempted to explain that my sleep plan was ruined, I was exhausted, I was dizzy, I just threw up in the shower, and diminutive cliffhangers were assembling on the shampoo rack. This proved to be a lot to swallow, and her motherly instincts were at their peak. To say that she was a worrier would be the understatement of the century, so hearing her son retelling tales from an obvious hallucination was unquestionably a cause for alarm.

Still, I refused to stay home. I had an important earth science exam, and nothing was going to keep me away from ski club. I tried, desperately, to pull myself together and get dressed. Another round of vomiting, stumbling, and banging into walls was followed by a long rest on the downstairs couch with cool compresses on my temples. I stayed there, attempting to regain my composure, until she came down to take me to school.

Mom was visibly anxious and strongly advised me against continuing the insanity. But I'm a stubborn soul, and the fact that I had a crucial exam played well to her educator instincts. I convinced her I would be fine by the afternoon and promised I'd take it easy during the day. I assured her I wouldn't attend the ski trip if I felt I might, in any way, endanger myself. She ultimately acquiesced and drove me to school.

During homeroom, I was introduced to the strange phenomenon of radically amplified hearing. As I sat at my desk, every pen drop, closing door, torn page, opened book, laugh, and whisper was deafening. I have always had highly acute hearing, but this was well beyond tolerable. I sat there, with my hands over my ears, and tried to endure the cacophony in the room. The class was a hazy blur, and my friends and fellow students chalked my odd behavior up to sickness. From an outsider's perspective, it wasn't overtly obvious that I was in any exceptional danger.

The next class was earth science, and my performance on that supposedly significant exam was laughable. I could barely focus on filling in the answer columns, let alone remember a fraction of anything we'd learned. Still, I plowed through the test with my sights firmly set on the night ahead. My utter oblivion was astounding. But it was my nature to set a steady focus and ignore any obstacles that prevented me from reaching my goals. It's a quality that generally served me well, but blindly bulldozing to the finish line is not always the smartest means of travel.

My physical pain was bad, but not unmanageable. As the day progressed, I believed I was getting better. I even managed to convince myself that I would be ready to rock by the time we loaded the ski bus. But during my fourth period class, I was unexpectedly called down to the main office to find Mom waiting to take me to my doctor.

Her proactivity was vital. The clock was clearly not running in my favor, and apparently, she was a lot more concerned than she appeared that morning. As I was in my fog, the diligent pragmatist was there to rescue and protect. Just as the body's central function is to monitor and regulate for survival, Mom's exclusive assignment was to keep me safe. This, she would often tell me, was the sole reason she was put on this earth. She gave me life and then spent every waking second ensuring that life was preserved.

Her eyes were determined, but comforting. I knew immediately that this was not a topic open for debate. But I couldn't grasp the concept of tragedy and trauma at that age, and my primary focus was on the slopes. Mom read that clearly. She even managed to assure me that everything was probably fine and that there was still a good chance I would make it back before the closing bell. She generally subscribed to the "better safe than sorry" doctrine, so we drove over to my physician's office for a quick evaluation. But I would never be on that bus.

THE GUESSING GAME

DURING OUR DRIVE to the office, the symptoms from earlier that morning were nearly nonexistent. The pressure in my head had equalized, my nausea subsided, and the dizziness was almost gone. It felt like I had turned a corner, so I assumed whatever bug or flu had attacked me was retreating. My situation seemed to be on the upswing, and I was fairly confident I would be given a clean bill of health. This is why I'm not a doctor.

The first of my many saviors was my pediatrician, Dr. P. She listened to our inexplicable tale of the morning's events and, like a true professional, snapped into action. After the standard lights in the eyes, ears, and throat routine, she asked me to do something that set into motion some strikingly consequential events.

I was told to stand in the corner with my eyes closed and my arms stretched out to my sides. I was then asked to turn my palms toward the ceiling. Immediately, I lost balance and stumbled backwards. This was very obviously not a normal response, and I felt the heaviness and weight of the room. There was a palpable tension that permeated the air. This was trouble.

I was reminded of a movie I saw a few years earlier where a man suffering from a brain tumor was given a similar test, with similar results. For the first time, I was struck with real fear. Questions started flooding my head, and my hands started to shake. This Friday was not going according to plan. The only concern I had that morning was missing a ski trip. Now, my survival hung in the balance? A thirteen-year-old boy is not ready to face life-and-death decisions. My world was about to go off the rails, and I wasn't prepared for the plummet.

Dr. P made some phone calls and wrote a prescription for a CT scan at our local hospital. She was calm and efficient, but there was an explicit sense of urgency in what she did. She had been my doctor since I was a baby, and it was clear she felt unsettled by what she saw. My insulated world of teenage security was quickly spinning out of control. We didn't know it then, but we were hurtling into the eye of the storm.

We arrived at the hospital with strangled nerves and a looming uncertainty of the future. Still, with few remaining symptoms, it didn't feel like I was ringing death's doorbell. I was physically getting better by the hour while my psychological state bore the brunt of the damage. The game plan was clear, and there was no way to escape the inevitable. It was time to learn the truth.

The CT scan was a new experience for me. I was always incredibly healthy, and despite my participation in various athletics, I had never suffered a broken bone or fracture of any kind. I'd had an X-ray before, but it was always during a routine dental exam. The CT scan carried with it a new physical environment as well as the added gravity of our mounting wariness.

The giant donut-shaped machine looked fairly intimidating. I was told to lie down on a body-sized track that would essentially pull me into the scanning area. Two Velcro straps at the forehead and chin locked me in place. My arms remained at my side, unfettered. My instructions were to stay as still as possible. Under no circumstances should I move my head. The slightest shift could make the scans unreadable. So I held my breath and didn't blink.

It has been well documented that memories triggered by our sense of smell can elicit authentic recreations of past events in our lives. This concept is particularly true for me, and the smell of that first scan planted a hefty memory marker in my brain. As the emitter and receiver circled my head, an odd metallic odor filled the scanning field. If anything even slightly resembles that smell, I am immediately transported back to that moment. I would guess that some type of traumatic scar was burned into my psyche that day. It was the first of many.

When I walked out of the room, a quick rush of pressure blurred my vision and knocked me off balance again. The rapid change in my position caused the dormant fluid to flow back into my head, and it was more than my body could manage. It was like being reminded of a paper cut or splinter. Everything felt fine until one particular movement. I realized I was still deep in the woods, but those sensibilities were driven more by bewilderment than fear.

The technician brought Mom into a smaller room adjacent to the waiting area. I was told to take a seat outside. The tech explained that the scans showed some excessive fluid on the brain, but he wouldn't know more details without further investigation. The results were given to Dr. P, and she was responsible for forming a plan of action. Mom had been uncharacteristically calm and attentive during this process, but the chinks in her armor presented themselves when her sister appeared at the end of the hall.

Mom had called Joyce earlier that morning to discuss the situation, but she never had a chance to give her any updates. So when my aunt arrived, the levee of emotions finally broke. She took one look at Joyce, one look back at her helpless son sitting alone in the hall, and all the worry and heartbreak she had been bottling up to appear strong erupted. The two embraced, each woman becoming a support beam for the other. Joyce didn't have any concrete information, but the strain in her sister's eyes spoke volumes.

Dr. P asked that Mom return to the office with the CT films. She'd gotten the verbal report from the hospital, but she wanted to visually examine them as well. So Mom and Joyce picked up some lunch and dropped me back at the house to rest. The office was very close to home, and I think they both needed a minute to process what had just transpired. They wiped away tears and headed over to Dr. P's with heavy scans and heavier hearts.

I walked around the house, very upset by the fact that I would definitely be missing ski club but more than happy I didn't have to suffer through the school day in pain. Still, I wrestled with an internal conflict because I wasn't overly symptomatic and I felt more than capable of tackling the mountain. The memories of the morning were fading, and at that point, I didn't have access to the same information that Mom and Joyce received. In hindsight, it was so much better that way. But it's hard to swallow disappointment, especially when you only see part of the picture.

When they returned to the house, I was given the abridged version of any "need to know" information, clinically and directly. I was told that Dr. P made some phone calls to Westchester Medical Center and we would be going there for the night. They wanted to do more testing, and some of the top doctors in the field would be seeing me.

So I went upstairs and gathered my things. The idea of being at the hospital for more than a night never really crossed my mind, so my bag was laughably light. I focused on the essentials, including wearing an old pair of sweatpants that brought me this strange sense of security. But I made absolutely sure to include plenty of music, which was my lifeblood and calming force. I brought some boxers and a few t-shirts. Only as an afterthought, I tossed in a couple of magazines, believing there would probably never be any time to read.

It makes almost no sense to me now, but I had an odd enthusiasm for embarking on this adventure. I guess that was proof of how little I really understood about the severity of my circumstances. I have always had some bizarre, energized reactions to times of tragedy. I would assume it stems from an adrenaline rush due to fear and uncertainty, but deviations in the schedules or rhythms of life fill me with excitement. I've regularly been infatuated with the latest car chase, media blitz, or natural disaster. It's just the way my body and mind process the overload. But with the questionable state of my health, that inclination waned quickly.

It took under an hour to make the drive to Westchester. I was tucked into the narrow backseat of a Celica, thinking about the unexpected surprises in life, and how the events of that Friday transpired. I could never have imagined heading to the hospital instead of the slopes. But I kept babbling about how our drive felt like a road trip or mini-vacation. Mom and Joyce, through the halfhearted smiles that hid their gripping panic, agreed. I looked up at the stars and got lost in adolescent thoughts.

THE REALIZATION

WE PULLED INTO the Westchester Medical Center parking lot. The grounds of the facility were huge, and it took some time to find the correct building. I gathered my small bag, double-checking that my headphones and CDs were still in order, and shuffled closely behind Mom and Joyce. I felt dwarfed next to the towering structure, and I was swallowed by the impending certainty that something exceptional was about to change.

The air had gotten considerably colder. It was only a short drive, but our suffocating nerves chilled us to the bone. We headed into the reception area of the ER to meet our contact, but apparently, there was a lot of action that night. The nurse at the front desk handed us a substantial volume of medical paperwork and asked us to take a seat in the waiting area.

Relaxing in that environment proved to be difficult. There was confusion, unfamiliar signals, and a general sense that we were in the way. Because I was a last-minute admission, we had to wait for my assigned room to become available.

We were brought into a larger holding area with multiple beds. This section was full of patients with varying ailments, and the sounds of suffering were painfully clear. Everyone needed assistance, and there was almost no way for the doctors to accommodate every request.

There was a young woman in the bed across from me enduring multiple spinal taps. The doctors weren't able to draw the desired amount of fluid so several attempts were necessary. She screamed in agony as the needles breached her spine. It became almost impossible to block out the sounds of her discomfort. I was more than anxious, and the physical reality of my environment was finally settling in. But it was obvious I was in much better shape than the majority of this assemblage.

Various nurses and members of the medical staff gave us regular updates about the doctor's status. Dr. R was still in surgery. Dr. R was checking on a patient in another building. Dr. R had to take an important phone call about a prospective procedure. Dr. R was called up to a different floor for a consultation.

In the meantime, a number of surgical residents appeared at the foot of my bed, asking the same questions, in the same manner. I politely recounted the day's details with fairly forced enthusiasm. I must have told my story twenty times that night. I became very comfortable with the script's broken record repetition. Then I got a visit from a member of Dr. R's surgical team.

I can't recall the name or face of this man. He had no definite shape or size. He wore no discernible smile or possessed any memorable physical attribute. If I had been asked to give a description, I would have sounded like a victim trying to recall the color and style of the shirt worn by his assailant. The doctor's face was a blur, and his words were a mix of noises from some twisted nightmare. But like a meteorologist delivering a weather report, he calmly and robotically detailed the many facets of my condition.

He explained the strategy for mounting an attack, and we listened with astonishment and disbelief. But his speech was so mechanically straightforward that we got sucked into this odd state of compliance. It was as if a man speaking Japanese was selling us his car, but because he was so emphatic and direct, we had no choice but to buy.

Here's the short version. The human brain has four ventricles that maintain the balance and flow of cerebrospinal fluid (CSF) in, out, and around the spine and cranium. These carefully regulated levels are absolutely essential in shielding the fragile brain inside the skull from shock or trauma. The CSF is in constant motion, moving up and down the spinal cord, and occupying the subarachnoid space and ventricular system around and inside the brain. The fluid also provides basic mechanical and immunological protection. So it's pretty essential that these quantities remain meticulously balanced.

The doctor explained that I had a condition known as hydrocephalus—from the Greek *hydro* meaning "water" and *kephalē* meaning "head"—which is sometimes referred to as water on the brain. I was vaguely familiar with the image of babies born with enlarged heads. But I always assumed this disorder primarily affected infants. We learned, however, that in some rare situations, the onset of hydrocephalus could occur later in life. I had a blockage, somewhere between the third and fourth ventricles, causing the CSF levels in my brain to rise at a threatening rate. At that time, there were few definitive conclusions about the origin or cause of my condition. But it was clear that immediate action was necessary.

I was so impressed with the way Mom handled everything. She refused to show any signs of fear or weakness. I was protected by my inexperience and a youthful sense of invincibility. But having just received word that her healthy only child had a life-threatening medical condition involving the strong possibility of a brain tumor, she snapped into "business mode" and began setting the necessary wheels in motion. Her strength was beyond belief. It's something I'll never forget.

Although the weight of this news was intense, it was impossible for me to absorb the significance of what I was told. I had no idea what it felt like to go through neurosurgery. I had no clue about the risks involved: blindness, brain damage, or death. I couldn't envision the incredible strength and willpower it takes to endure days of immobility. I was unaware of how quickly every muscle in the body, especially the legs, loses strength and flexibility. I couldn't predict the overwhelming lack of self-esteem, loss of confidence, traumatic scars, and all-encompassing body insecurities that would plague me for the rest of my life. This was merely the first step of the marathon. No one has written a handbook for this kind of thing.

Shortly after the bomb drop, we met Dr. R for the first time. She was a confident tiny woman with a direct, forceful nature that demanded attention and respect. Mom had a tough time trying to make sense of her in the beginning because Dr. R was much more interested in my personal story and interpretation of what had happened. She wasn't exactly receptive to Mom's plethora of questions and concerns. She may not have been warm and fuzzy, but it was clear she was efficient. Since my life was on the line, I preferred the latter. We could worry about hugs and smiles when I was out of the woods.

Our introduction was brief, and Dr. R was whisked away to another task. We were then told that a bed in the step-down unit was open. Patients in step-down weren't well enough for private rooms, but they didn't require the constant surveillance of the ICU. It served only as a temporary rest area for me, but it was better than floating in limbo.

It was nice to have my own bed, but the atmosphere in step-down was dramatically different. Many patients were hooked up to monitoring devices, and the majority was sleeping or too weak to communicate. The chaotic environment of the ER was replaced with a serene calm. At least the ER sounded alive. This felt like cold storage for the bedridden. I looked around at the row of patients and, for the first time, registered the upsetting prospects of my future. It was unthinkable that I could be reduced to such crippling weakness, but the inevitability of the road ahead was finally clear. I put on some Bob Marley and tried to drift away from my thoughts.

In the morning, I heard the pathetically funny tale of Mom and Joyce's makeshift shower experience and lounge chair sleeping exploits. A little humor was exactly what I needed. They knew how to paint a smile on my face, even in the darkest moments.

Incredibly, Mom spent every single night in that hospital with me. This was merely the first test of her resilience. Her patience and endurance were heavily strained, but she just rolled over the speed bumps. Every new obstacle or piece of disheartening news was met with studied attention and an emphasis on positivity. She was a rock when I was a willow in the wind. This extraordinary low-maintenance gene was certainly not something I inherited. My two warrior women eventually left to find coffee downstairs, so I put on my headphones and flipped through some magazines. Then, without warning, my father appeared from around the corner.

It's important to shed some background on the history of this paternal relationship. My parents were separated when Mom got pregnant, and they divorced shortly after. I spent my weekends with Paul until I started playing soccer on Saturdays when I was eight. We never cultivated any real father-son bond, and I often resented the times I was pulled away from friends to fulfill my visitation obligations. When my weekends became occupied, he made very little effort to play a significant part in my life. I didn't do much on my end to include him, so some of the blame was on both of us. I was an only child with a single parent. That was the only world I knew. The psychological repercussions from my abandonment issues wouldn't affect me until much later. I kept my focus on Mom, school, friends, girls, music, and sports. That was enough to fill my hard drive.

Mom felt that notifying Paul of my situation was the right thing to do despite our total lack of contact in the previous few years. The one stipulation was that he was not to come to the hospital under any circumstances. I wasn't in the right frame of mind to open that can of worms, so he agreed to keep his distance. Apparently, when Paul agreed to something, it didn't mean much.

Seeing his face staring back at me was surreal. His image was like a mirage, and I couldn't wrap my head around the fact that he was actually standing there. He sheepishly walked over to my bed and took a seat. Both of us were nervous, and the current climate didn't make things any easier. There was some forced small talk, but we slowly settled into each other's company. I had some mixed emotions because I didn't want to see him, but the fact that he cared enough to be part of my support system was admirable.

My grandparents had also come to visit, and they ran into Mom and Joyce in the hallway outside my room. Grandma admitted she granted Paul access to see me, and she believed her behavior was justified. Mom was less than thrilled, but when she saw that I was okay, she relaxed. It was about to be one big awkward family affair. Some patients never received any visitors. They watched the clock spin in isolation. I was fortunate to have people who were willing to put in those long hospital hours. There would be plenty of alone time in my future, so I was happy to have the company.

I spent one more night in step-down, and then I was moved to a room on the pediatric floor. I felt more comfortable having a centralized setup. It was much easier to accommodate visitors, and I was away from the severity and quietude of the step-down environment. My symptoms were subdued at that point, and all my youthful energy had returned. I was mugging for the camera and acting like a kid at sleepaway camp. I was still blind to the impending storm, but I instinctively went into escape mode to preserve my sanity.

My new roommate, Stevie, had some serious troubles, and the fluid trapped in his lungs kept him coughing and suffering each night. He was younger than me, and his life expectancy was drastically reduced by his condition. He became a rooted reminder that we were residents of a home for the sick, and sometimes the sick can't be healed.

For the next two days, I was subjected to multiple CT scans, MRI (magnetic resonance imaging) scans, and various picks, pokes, and prods. One of the more unpleasant experiences was the changing of my IV. An IV catheter in the arm has to be swapped every two or three days to avoid clogging and infection. However, I happened to have thick skin, and I was referred to as a "hard stick." Whenever they tried to insert the line into my vein, they often had complications. Once, I was woken in the middle of the night because my IV had stopped. It took three nurses and four attempts to finally establish a drip. Also, my veins had a tendency to "pop." This is when the placement of the IV renders the vein useless or causes a spurt of blood to shoot back out of the insertion site. It's not pretty, and it's not for the squeamish. I dreaded that catheter change.

I met with an ophthalmologist who determined that I had a slight swelling of the optic nerve called papilledema. The increased fluid inside my head put added stress on the nerve, causing acute sensitivity to light and an extended blind spot. Papilledema is not a permanent condition, and the symptoms were supposed to subside when the pressure normalized.

I also completed a neuropsychology evaluation. This series of tests determined the proper steps necessary for the rehabilitation of patients who suffered illness or injury to the brain. They looked at cerebral pathology and the correlation between brain illnesses and psychological factors. I knew very little about why certain questions were asked, but I answered each one with supreme confidence and I was pleased with my performance. The fact that I thought this test was based on aptitude or somehow rewarded my capacity to respond correctly was another example of my oblivious teenage perspective.

After another round of scans, we were told that the cause of my blockage could be a water-based cyst or just some variant of my anatomy. The doctors explained that they would be able to offer a more concrete assessment after surgery. The likelihood that it was a tumor, malignant or benign, was highly remote. But we took a big collective breath and hoped for the latter.

The scheduled procedure was the placement of a ventriculoperitoneal (VP)—from the Latin *ventriculus* meaning "ventricles" and Greek *peri* meaning "around" and *teiein* "to stretch"—shunt, which is a system that "shunts" or redirects the flow of CSF from the brain to another area of the body where it can be absorbed. The shunt is a soft, flexible, sturdy elastic tube. It's usually composed of polymeric silicone, which is compatible with human body tissues. One end of the catheter is placed inside the ventricle and the other end is directed into the abdominal cavity. A valve situated alongside the catheter maintains one-way flow and regulates the stream of CSF. This valve is positioned outside of the skull, just beneath the skin, and contains a flexible flushing chamber. If necessary, the chamber permits the removal of CSF by a physician using a syringe. It also allows the shunt to be flushed by pumping the chamber to send fluid toward or away from the ventricles. This can help the doctor to determine if the system is functioning properly. But during normal operation, the valve is designed to maintain a balanced fluid level without any intervention.

The night before the surgery, the game changed. For the first time, the realization of what I was about to face became frighteningly clear. I shed the happy, lighthearted exterior, took off my mask of bravery, and sat inside the weight of the moment. Fear and hesitation smothered me in a cyclone of apprehension. It was the most intense mix of emotions I'd ever experienced. The very real prospects of injury, blindness, neurological trauma, or death finally hit me. I don't know if I was lying to myself or simply being strong in front of my visitors, but the culmination of five days of physical and psychological turmoil ruptured my emotional dam. The floodgates opened.

I was a thirteen-year-old boy confronting my mortality. There was something inherently unnatural about that, and my cognitive core began to morph into something new. This consciousness set the foundation for a divergence of roads. When the order of the universe is disrupted, the individuals affected are forever changed. Parents never recover from losing their offspring. An abused child never forgets the pain. Deep cerebral scars are formed that can't completely heal, despite how much time passes. I didn't know it then, but I was about to take my first step toward living a life hanging in the balance.

THE TRANSFORMATION

I WOKE UP on surgery morning exhausted from the brutal night. A new IV solution was started, and I spent the first hour drifting in and out of sleep. The fact that I was so tired helped dull the day's nerves. I was more than happy to let the haze of insomnia keep me away from the swirling, racing thoughts.

A nurse came to take me to the operating room (OR) a little before noon. I had a procession of well-wishers, including my aunts, uncles, grandparents, Mom, and Paul. They populated the waiting area, holding vigil and attempting to preserve their sanity. There was enough concentrated positive energy in that room to heal the entire floor.

When I was wheeled into the OR, I spoke briefly to the anesthesiologist and Dr. R before succumbing to the power of artificial sleep. Shortly before going under, an odd sense of calm enveloped me. I had finally let my mind and muscles surrender to their fate. I don't believe it was the drugs as much as a natural human instinct to seek health and repair. I put my faith and life in the hands of a specialist and closed my eyes.

The surgery lasted about two hours, and I was brought to recovery at 3:00 p.m. They found no tumor or cyst, but an excessive amount of fluid was loitering inside my skull, uninvited. I was barely alert enough to speak to Mom for a minute, and the first words I uttered were "I need a hug." My body felt like it had been smashed by a Mack truck, so I quickly fell into a well-earned rest. Soon after, I was given a post-op X-ray and taken to my room.

I was back in my bed around 6:00 p.m., much more awake and aware of my physical state. There was a large bandage covering the right side of my head, and two smaller dressings shielded my collarbone and abdomen. I was swollen and stiff. Only half of my head was shaved, and when I felt the dissymmetry, my stomach sank. I understood that removing the hair was a surgical necessity, so I urged the doctors to crop everything. Unfortunately, in order to maintain a sanitary environment, that was impossible. This discovery probably affected me more than it should have, but I was trying so desperately to hold on to some semblance of my former identity. The only control I had was physical. It was simply a way to take an avalanche and make it a snowball. That night, the last remaining hope of sliding through this situation unscathed was perfectly abolished.

I tossed and turned, unable to rest under the pain of fresh wounds. I was given Tylenol with codeine, and after I vomited, the doctor assumed I was allergic. My frustration grew while my patience waned. The feeling of inescapable discomfort was one of the most grueling sensations. It was a measured form of torture. Immobility and insomnia heightened the intensity. But I was about to learn what it was like to live in a cage of my own body.

The next morning marked the start of my forty-eight-hour movement restriction. In order for the system to acclimate, there could be no drastic fluctuations in intracranial pressure. I had to remain in a reclined, almost flat pose until my doctors deemed it safe to adjust. The changes in elevation were made in 15° intervals, and they couldn't come fast enough. Lying there in that prone position, with no ability to sit, stand, or alter my posture, was hell. My muscles were weak, my wounds were sore, and I felt this overwhelming impulse to run out of my skin. I was locked in a restricted movement prison.

The only respite came from the various trips to the scanning area. But even the slightest activity was strenuous and slow. I was overcome by bouts of dizziness, and my limbs were as lax as a ragdoll's. These short periods out of bed were blaring indicators that I needed more days to heal. Every injury has a recovery period, but the brain is the motherboard of the entire system. When the circuits get fried, it takes considerably more effort to reboot.

After I was raised another 15°, I was hopeful I would be released in a couple of days. But Dr. R felt that because of the severity of the wounds, coupled with my age, she should keep me there a while longer for observation. She explained that the soreness was to be expected and that my body had basically undergone a beating. I never sensed anything less than confidence and support from her. The work was done, and this was all just a part of the recuperation.

I tried to eat for the first time in a couple of days, and I attempted to rest whenever possible. I was given permission to turn onto my side, which helped ease the discomfort. My strength was returning slowly, and I got accustomed to my surroundings and more accepting of my limitations. The human body has a remarkable ability to adjust and adapt. My anxiety eased, and I did my best to manage the stiffness. Pills and painkillers never really agreed with my system, so I utilized more mental coping mechanisms. A combination of music, emotional displacement, and positive thinking worked wonders.

We had a slight scare one morning when we were told that a test of my CSF revealed some type of germ. It was analyzed to determine a possible infection because the test showed an increase in white corpuscles. The doctors reassured us, claiming they weren't concerned, but they planned to monitor any increase in temperature or severity of headaches. This was not the news we wanted to hear, but it was merely one more detail beyond our control. At that point, we'd gotten pretty familiar with our roles as passengers, not drivers. So we quietly hoped for the best.

Mom had practically moved into the hospital. She slept in shifts, tended to my needs, and tried desperately to get answers out of doctors who were far more interested in what I had to say. Her stamina was shocking. I still don't understand how someone wrought with such immense stress could muster enough strength to put on a face and pretend things were fine. She endured more worry and fear than any human being should suffer, and I owe my life to her diligence and unwavering support.

She passed endless hours journaling, documenting my struggles and tiny triumphs, and attempting to maintain some ounce of sanity by pouring her pain onto the page. As luck would have it, there were actually a couple of instances when a five-minute trip to the cafeteria caused her to miss a visit by the doctor or the chance to get some valuable piece of information from a nurse. I was usually in no condition to comprehend everything, so she often returned to the room visibly disheartened. Mom assumed the duty of overseeing the base camp. We lived in a world beyond our control, so focusing on me and my immediate needs helped her maintain a sense of peace and perspective.

My elevation remained static at 15°. When I was lifted to 30°, my CSF drained too quickly. So I stayed at a reduced incline to avoid any complications. When the bed was raised again, I was dizzy and had to return to my original position. It was a precarious balance, but the best barometer was my body's response to the fluctuations and my physical endurance for each setting. It was a repetitive, often deflating dance.

For the next few days, I rested, continued to regain my strength, and tested my tolerance for the increased elevation. I even sat up at 60° and played some cards with Grandpa. The lightheadedness returned whenever I looked up or tilted my neck, but I pushed myself to take as much pain and discomfort as safely possible. Any progress in rehabilitation took that extra effort. My personality never allowed me to roll over and play dead.

Walking was a challenge. It was shocking how quickly the muscles weakened. I had only been lying in bed for eight days, but my legs were gelatin. I actually did a pretty decent Bambi impression on my first trip down the hallway. My knees buckled, I lost balance, and I moved like a snail on ice. I could empathize with patients who were bedridden for any significant length of time. It was a slow, dispiriting retraining process. But muscle memory is a powerful gift, and our bodies can find their way back. The will to push through the torpid pace was the challenge.

The stitches were removed, and the top of my head radiated heat like an oven. The sensation was similar to scabs being ripped from a wound. There were thirty-seven sutures in my head, four at my collarbone, and eight on my stomach. It was necessary to utilize these other incision sites so the shunt could be properly threaded along the neck, past the collarbone, and into the abdominal cavity. A misguided shunt would potentially cause drainage problems and various other complications. Oddly, the stomach incision was more tender than the lacerations on my head. This was probably because some nerve endings were damaged on the skull. An area of my abdominal wall had to be breached for shunt insertion, so the pain in that zone was more intense. After the sutures were removed, one of the residents said I would probably be discharged the following day.

I woke with the sun, anxious to be free of the hospital walls. As expected, there was a delay getting my official paperwork, and we had to wait for Grandpa to arrive. Mom left to make a phone call, and I sat in bed processing the events of the last twelve days. I was gripped by a strange mix of jubilation and panic. I couldn't be more ready to return to reality, but the safety net of the hospital and the living angels who healed and nursed me back to life would be gone. It was terrifying.

There was so much unfamiliar ground waiting to be traversed. I was reassured but given no guarantees. My life now depended on the proper functioning of a synthetic mechanism in my head. The certainty of my health was undeniably out of my hands. Unless I somehow managed to puncture or break the tubing, there was nothing I could do to adversely or positively affect my condition. I wasn't able to siphon excess fluid or force the valve to regulate my CSF. Shunt systems can last a lifetime or break down in days. There was no possible way to predict their functionality or how specific systems would interact with certain individuals. The stopwatch had started, and I could only hope for a good run.

The playful, innocent boy who walked into that facility was not the wounded man who wobbled out. For the first time, I saw the world with new eyes. I gained perspective, experience, and an understanding of the relationship between life and death. Surrounded by pain and suffering, I discovered what it takes to rise above our limitations. I saw moments of despair and moments of triumph. I felt the most pure form of gratitude and respect for my protectors. I learned about fragility, love, and how beautiful we all are, even in our darkest moments. I figured out how to bleed and how to heal. I was human. I was alive.

THE HOMECOMING

EVERYTHING FELT NEW. I walked through my house like a curious puppy exploring his new terrain. All the familiar sounds, smells, and rigid schedules of the bustling hospital floor had vanished. I was able to move around freely, but any opportunity to take advantage of that privilege was a challenge. I was substantially weakened from the lack of activity and loss of weight, but the mental exhaustion played an even bigger role. Plus, I had the added hurdle of navigating foreign obstacles like carpeting and stairs. Everything took a little longer and seemed a little farther than I remembered. Also, the only bathroom was on the second floor, so I had to stockpile my stamina and schedule my treks accordingly.

Life in a hospital room is thoroughly insulated. The external world seems to stop. There is very little attention paid to news, current events, or the maintenance of any relationships outside the immediate family. Ironically, the vast spaces of time lend themselves well to work, reading, or writing. But the solitary focus on health and fear tramples any desire to fill the mind with peripheral interests or distractions. There are numerous stories of family members remaining at the bedside of a loved one for countless days, weeks, or months. Minutes seem to strangely stand still and disappear at the same time. It's hard to fully understand this phenomenon unless you've logged some hours in the waiting game.

When I was allowed to go home, it was a relief to sleep in familiar sheets, wake up of my own accord, and let the soothing images of my childhood soak into my consciousness. I still felt a persistent apprehension being away from the control center, but I tried to keep my focus on health and rehabilitation. The first few days were an adjustment, but I quickly fell back into my routine.

I stayed at home for a week and then returned to junior high, on a half-day basis. My barber, Dave, allowed me to come into his salon after hours so he could shave the other half of my head. He knew how uncomfortable I was with my physical appearance, and having a somewhat normal haircut helped make my transition a little less embarrassing. The conspicuous scars were another story.

Home tutoring was also a supplemental part of the plan. Four patient, competent instructors helped me recover the lost weeks and regain my academic stride. The accelerated math/science curriculum that year was difficult, so a lengthy absence from the classroom environment slowed my absorption rate. But I focused my efforts and found the challenge a motivator rather than a burden. Sadly, it wouldn't be the only occasion this pilot needed some extra fuel to make up time in the air.

I continued attending half-day classes for about a week and then returned to school, full-time. Dr. R sent a physical activity form detailing which sports were acceptable for participation, noting that my energy levels were compromised by the procedure. I was permitted to take part in almost every activity—excluding athletics that could jeopardize the head or neck, like football, wrestling, specific gymnastics, etc. Skiing was one sport that Dr. R verbally authorized, but my relatives took that permission a bit too literally.

For some incredibly odd reason, a family ski trip to Vermont with my aunt, uncle, and cousins seemed like a brilliant idea. We rarely traveled or took vacations, so an opportunity to leave for a few days was enticing. I suppose the original concept was a return to normalcy, but hitting the slopes less than a month after brain surgery didn't exactly turn out as we had hoped.

From the first run, it was obvious my beaten body was not prepared for the physical rigors of skiing. Mentally, I was ready to race with the pack and bury myself in powder, but my legs lacked the strength needed for turning and stopping. My wounds were still fresh, and my stomach muscles were weak. I kept pace with the crew for the first half of the run, but a sudden wave of exhaustion hit me like a sledgehammer and I had to take a seat in the middle of the mountain. I attempted to start down again and ran smack into a bright orange "Watch for Blind Skiers" flag marker. The irony was inescapable.

I was frustrated by my lack of agility and embarrassed by my performance. I knew I was a better skier than that, and I wanted to show my family I could pick up exactly where I left off. But sometimes even the most determined will cannot overcome physical restrictions. This was a lesson I needed to learn multiple times. Stubborn and unbending, I hated failing at anything. The control freak in me had a hard time being told no.

That ski trip was a wake-up call, but it was also a motivator. Although I wasn't able to rebound as quickly as I assumed I could, the fact that I was even on the mountain was a testament to my fighting spirit. I never saw the procedure as a handicap, and I stayed determined in my quest for a normal life. I understood the significance of everything I had endured, but I was fairly certain that it was behind me. There was a clog in my brain, a doctor installed some hardware to fix the issue, and that was it. Case closed.

My hair grew back. My strength returned. My wounds healed and shrank. I fell back into the folds of school, sports, music, and girls. I remained acutely aware of my artificial rubber inhabitants, but my activities were largely unaffected. My mind felt clearer, I had fewer headaches, and my vision improved almost instantly. Bizarrely, I even added skateboarding and snowboarding to my recreational checklist. Six months after the procedure, there were no conspicuous indicators that anything was different. In the world of hydrocephalus, I was an anomaly.

This fact was clear to Dr. R as well. A few months after another excellent follow-up exam, Mom received a call from the mother of a boy who had recently undergone a shunt implantation. The worried woman explained that her son was simply not coping with his situation. He hated the fact that something was in his body; he wore a hat at all times to cover the scars and pronounced valve, and he had fallen into a slight depression. Dr. R recommended that this woman and her son speak to me, since I was an example of a patient who was assimilating well to his hardware. Unfortunately, it was difficult to set the boy's worries to rest. All of us handle adversity in different ways. There were more variables at play than just a shared procedure. A lack of confidence or self-esteem is lethal to the healing process. The psychological scars can be much deeper than the physical ones. Neurosurgical patients have to learn self-repair from the inside out.

We are incredibly fragile creatures. One piece of news. One minute. One day. This can send us reeling. There is no such thing as genuine security. The healthiest fall ill, and the strongest crumble. Living in a bubble is protective only if we refuse to believe in the reality of the outside world. True awakening comes from pain and the triumph felt from its defeat. I lived under the illusion that I could return to society unscathed. I believed my surgery was merely a speed bump on a journey of self-discovery. But the real growth came from the fight.

THE WARNING SIGNS

MY ADOLESCENCE CONTINUED in a fairly normal fashion. Braces came off my teeth, a driver's license found its way into my wallet, my teenage heart was broken and mended, and I was able to maintain the tricky balance of personal independence with the security of home. Friends were tight. School was never an issue. Life was good.

I always pushed to stay on par with everyone else. I never shied away from a challenge, mental or physical, and I conducted myself like a typical teen. Still, I was careful about any headlocks or pressure around my neck, yelling, "Shunt! Shunt!" whenever I was involved in a little roughhousing. It became a running joke with my inner circle, but everyone respected my condition and treated me well. My assimilation into the world was complete. I relaxed and enjoyed the ride. Then, almost three years to the date, I found myself sitting in Dr. R's office discussing my options.

I had been having some intermittent headaches for almost two weeks, and I suspected there might be something wrong with my neurological plumbing. These headaches were not from stress, eyestrain, or hunger. They felt different. I became aware of that heavy, clogged sensation again. To preserve my sanity, I convinced myself the shunt was fine, but logic disagreed.

Dr. R ordered an MRI the day before my appointment. I studied the films and, in my "expert" medical opinion, concluded that the system was functioning properly. There wasn't a noticeable fluid increase, the ventricles looked normal, and there seemed to be little variation from the previous scans. However, I was sixteen years old and far from receiving a medical degree. But my assessment was actually somewhat correct.

There was not an excessive amount of fluid in the ventricles, but the valve's flushing chamber felt a little stiffer and more resistant than normal. This was not an immediate cause for alarm, and Dr. R noted that protein buildup could temporarily clog the chamber. This would explain my headaches and the unusually firm hardware.

I was given instructions to manually pump the valve twice a day, keeping a journal to record fluctuations in the duration and intensity of my headaches. The idea of pushing the spongy chambers of my valve was disconcerting, but I did as I was told. I don't know if the relief was genuine or merely psychosomatic, but the headaches lessened. Plus, I now had a new activity I could obsess about to help regain control of my own body. This was a dangerous discovery.

The doctor also remarked that the generous buildup of protein could be the cause of my frequent neck and abdominal discomfort. Whenever I stretched my body and arms to reach for a rebound or jump in the air for an overhead in tennis, I could sense the strain on the shunt. It never felt like it would snap, but the muscles surrounding the tubing got sore and stiff. It could take a whole day for total flexibility to return. This was a problem that consistently plagued me, occurring without any real warnings. It was wildly sporadic. The same activity on a different day could yield contrasting results.

But any stiffness was just an inconvenience, and this newfound pumping technique set my mind at ease. Still, the crack in the dam was exposed. This was not a flawless system, and my body's specific chemistry seemed to adversely affect its function. On my path of continuous education about hydrocephalus and shunting, this was a revelation. My perception of any real control vanished to an even greater extent. The countdown had begun.

Dr. R ordered a more detailed set of X-rays called a shunt series. These helped give a better view of the location and positioning of the tubing, and they revealed if any kinks or tears were affecting the flow. Issues with the actual shunt were unlikely. Apparently, I would have had more severe symptoms than mild headaches if the tube had any material complications.

A call came from the doctor's office the next day. The shunt series was normal. So thoughts of any hiccups with the placement of the tube and valve were dismissed. This left only one feasible conclusion. My body's excessive protein production was clogging my valve and causing the system to break down.

Dr. R never put this into words, but I saw the writing on the wall. I didn't fully vocalize my worries, so Mom just considered this process another bullet dodged. She was happy that the scans were good and thankful there wasn't a larger issue on the table. Unfortunately, the obsessive king in the castle of my mind disagreed.

This office visit marked the first time that the possibility of malfunction was a concern. Something that I believed would last a lifetime was now showing signs of operational error less than three years after its introduction. I was shaken, and any faith I had in the concept of preserving some notion of absolute health vanished. I could pump that valve at the first sign of a headache until my fingers were raw, but eventually, it would cease to perform its task. Now, it was simply a question of when.

THE ROLLER COASTER CLIMB

LIFE CONTINUED ON track. High school was under control. Friends were always there. I learned how to love and how to lose, but the future loomed. The college quest began. I started aligning my ducks in neatly organized rows. I savored my freedom but buckled down when appropriate. It was a perfect coming-of-age story, with a twist. I was a normal teenager with a ticking time bomb.

My skin wrapped itself around the synthetic tubing, pretending to welcome the invasion. The shunt system was an assimilated part of my lifestyle, but it was never entirely accepted. I lived under the guise of faux functionality, but it was impossible to hide from the hovering storm clouds. My mind didn't allow me to disengage, so there wasn't a day that I didn't think about that shunt. I couldn't go anywhere without being keenly aware of its presence and inescapability. Still, I defied its grip on my world. Even with the faint cry of warning sirens, I always believed I could control my destiny. But I was taught a painful lesson about dangerous expectations and the futility of trying to orchestrate fate.

I finished high school and headed to Ithaca to study communications and learn the invaluable lessons of collegiate life. I was only three hours from base camp, but the extraction of my security blanket made the distance feel much farther. I learned to cope with a roommate, juggle increased academic responsibilities, and maintain my focus amid a barrage of social distractions. It was a new world, and I was willing and ready to accept the challenge.

Freshman year is a significant milestone in the life of a young adult. It's during this time that a bridge between boyhood and manhood is built. These worlds are often in opposition, so the real test is trying to make peace with two warring sides in an attempt to meet in the middle. The boy holds tightly to a life of memories while the man looks for the next adventure and a malleable future. It's like the molting of old skin, and the process is wrought with confusion.

I was one of the lucky souls to have made that transition with few stumbling blocks. My first year was a perfect exercise in growth. New friends took the place of old, and the seeds for the continuous evolution of my life were planted. I flourished in a world of self-discovery, and the introduction of heavy introspection played a crucial role in my psychological health. I didn't know it then, but the troops were convening and planning their attack. My cage was about to get rattled, and my sanity's delicate balance would be tested to its limits.

I had maintained a relationship with my high school girlfriend, Keish, and we planned on continuing indefinitely. She visited me in Ithaca a number of times during my freshman year, and we did our best to navigate new waters. The foundation of our dynamic was built on peaks and valleys, but the added stress of distance didn't help. Still, we reunited when I came home that summer and attempted to pick things up where they had paused.

It felt so comfortable to have her back at my side. Through all the little spats and disagreements, we were a great team. She was a bearer of unconditional love, but soaked in stubbornness and youth, I refused to acknowledge how special and rare that was. Life and age would hand me some valuable lessons, but a nineteen-year-old college kid is far too busy getting in his own way to appreciate what he's given.

We spent all of our time together and slipped back into a routine. Our days were filled with work and mini-adventures, and we fell into each other every night. Visits with old friends were sprinkled with stories from our respective battlefields. There was never competition, just a shared interest in each other's lives. We even made a few trips to the shore to hang with some of my Ithaca true blues. It was a melding of the new and the old, and I couldn't be happier. Being back home was layered with memories of all that was and an anticipation for everything still to come. Then, the headaches began.

I had felt some increased pressure for two or three days in the last week of June. I wasn't losing sleep or fighting to hold my balance on the stairs, but something was definitely off. Then I woke up one morning, and my color was bad. The intensity of the pain had heightened, and I knew it was time to take a drive.

We made the trip down to Westchester with unsteady hands holding tightly to positive thinking. Because Dr. R had already given her "manual pumping" instructions, we hoped there was another quick-fix penny left for the wishing well. It was too disheartening to think about being painted into another corner. I had healed, made peace with the limitations of my condition, and was ready to author a new chapter in my life.

My mind was racing with memories of the incredibly lengthy and arduous recovery process that accompanied neurosurgery, and I was flooded with questions about the future. I couldn't imagine being subjected to that struggle and the rigors of the recuperation period again. How was I supposed to stay on track with my studies? Would I even be able to reenter the folds of college life? How terrible would I look? Things were going so well, but this might send me right back to the starting line. Plus, if the shunt system could break down so easily, what would that mean for my long-term health and sense of security? I didn't want to walk on the dark side, but complex scenarios escort complex worries. It wasn't a rainbows and daffodils kind of day.

We met with Dr. R, and she immediately diagnosed a shunt malfunction. She attempted to alleviate the fluid buildup by manually depressing the valve, but it was futile. It was clogged and rendered useless. My excessive protein levels struck again. This time, they went for the kill. It was all too much to process. This was the very definition of a worst-case scenario.

Dr. R then informed us about a procedure that was seemingly tailor-made for my condition. An operation called an endoscopic third ventriculostomy opens a new waterway inside the brain to circumvent blockages and eliminate the need for shunting altogether. There were fewer neurosurgeons qualified to perform this procedure, and that number was even smaller when I was first shunted. Actually, no surgeon at Westchester Medical was certified to execute a third ventriculostomy at that time. But had it been an available option, I might never have undergone shunting in the first place.

The third ventriculostomy is a high-risk procedure, but the benefits of successful completion far outweigh the dangers. For this surgery, a tiny burr hole is made in the skull, and a neuroendoscope (a small camera attached to a medical instrument) is used to enter the cranial cavity. The camera can view specific areas of the brain as well as the blockage site. A laser is employed to make another hole, several millimeters wide, in the floor of the third ventricle. The size of the hole is then dilated to create a detour around the blockage. This allows the CSF to flow from the blocked ventricles into the open spaces surrounding the brain. The fluid bypassing the blockage enables the system to function normally, absorbing and regulating the CSF as necessary.

It sounded like a miracle cure, and I felt the early pangs of anxiety and excitement. If everything went well, I would be able to see the world through a new set of eyes. The idea of freedom from the physical and emotional baggage of this condition was like a shiny lure at the end of a very long line. I knew the ultimate prize, but there was a lot to consider. Was the hope of a new life worth the heavier risks of blindness, memory loss, or death? These were substantial stakes, and there wasn't room to waver.

We tried to digest all this new information to make an educated choice. The increasing fluid levels made it nearly impossible for me to focus or stay alert. The body went into a dormant, protective state when the intracranial pressure reached a certain degree. It's difficult to explain, but the effects are similar to staying up all night reading or attempting to concentrate on a monotonous lecture. Needless to say, I wasn't much help in the decision-making process. So with few options, less time, and the hope of an ultimate remedy, we were bound for Manhattan.

At Beth Israel, we were introduced to Dr. A, and I felt relatively comfortable with my first impression of him. He explained the procedure in greater detail, and he appeared methodical and capable. He was part of a team that touted one of the world's most renowned neurosurgeons, so I was confident this facility would be able to handle a surgery of this complexity.

I continued to fight off sleep as he looked over my scans and medical history. He even asked me if I'd ever traveled to South America, hypothesizing that the small blockage in my ventricle could have grown from some form of foreign parasite. But he was fairly confident it was just an anatomical flaw or random growth, and since I had never been off the East Coast, our neighbors to the south were probably not to blame. Because a malfunctioning shunt leaves little room for delay, I was scheduled for surgery the following morning.

I endured a night of relentless vital checks, but my outright exhaustion helped me fall back to sleep quickly after each interruption. The neuro exams were crucial given my physical state. Ironically, I wasn't administered any steroids to keep the pressure and swelling down. A third ventriculostomy requires a certain level of excess fluid. This enables the surgeon to map out the course of attack more easily. It's almost impossible to successfully perform the operation on a healthy individual with normal CSF levels.

My girlfriend and my aunt drove down to the city together in the morning. Keish was working for Joyce that summer, babysitting my cousins, so it was a comfortable relationship. They arrived just before I was taken to the OR, but I was able to squeeze a short visit into my last few available minutes. It wasn't a comfortable time, and the thoughts and projections of everything ahead made it a little tough to be social. But I appreciated their compassion and the extra effort they made to see me.

Consistent care was a major factor in my healing process, and without the strength and devotion of those three women, I would have been hopelessly lost. They were a triangle of positivity, efficiency, and love. They complemented each other perfectly and understood my need for a balanced support system.

The nurses wheeled me down the hall, and my mind went to all the familiar places. There was still a certain degree of disbelief, but the prospect of a "normal" body helped quell my nerves and allowed me to focus on the future. I can't say I wasn't afraid. But the uncertainty of the process, coupled with a consistent buildup of head pressure, made for some interesting tangential thoughts. It's amazing what images the brain can produce under distress. Still, I put my faith in the hands of a skilled neurosurgeon, closed my eyes, and hoped that I would see the world again.

I did. The procedure lasted a little less than two hours, and the results were positive. Dr. A reported that I actually had a fifth ventricle, or a smaller cavity that was functioning similarly to the standard four. He was also able to take a miniscule sample of the blockage for a biopsy. It was proposed that I had a glioma, which is a type of tumor that originates in the brain or spine. But the mass was so small that removing the blockage could have potentially created a scar larger than the tumor itself. Plus, the location was so precarious that no instrument or laser could safely perform an extraction without the threat of serious complications. The biopsy confirmed that the glioma was benign, so one box of worries fell from the shelf. But I still had a pretty full pantry.

I was taken to the step-down unit immediately following the procedure, and I stayed there for observation overnight. A catheter was placed in my brain for drainage, but it was scheduled to be removed a couple of days later. I slept and recovered, so thankful it was over but completely unaware of my physical body. I simply let the waves of exhaustion and medication take control. Step-down was just a haze of blinking lights and chirping monitor alerts. I'd face my realities in the morning.

I was put back in my original room. My compulsive nature rejoiced. The little comforts and familiarities meant so much when everything else was out of control. I finally became conscious of my body, and I took inventory of the damages. There was some significant soreness at both incision sites. Dr. A made one opening to perform the ventriculostomy and another to remove my valve.

The fact that it was gone was almost impossible to believe. The right side of my skull was smooth and hospitable, free of the spongy-humped intruders. It was a beautiful recollection. The familiar feel of a cranium I thought I'd lost was almost surreal. I went to sleep in a defined physical state and then woke up altered. The time lapse was erased under anesthesia, so the shock was even more pronounced. I was given light painkillers and medicine to reduce swelling.

Dr. A came to check on me, and he assumed everything was fine. Apparently, I would have been very sick if there wasn't a consistent CSF stream allowing the newly created detour to remain open. He planned on removing the drainage catheter the following morning, giving me another MRI to verify the flow, and then discharging me shortly after. I didn't feel great. But I'm a slow healer, so I blamed it on the bruises. That was one conclusion I shouldn't have leapt.

After the MRI, it was determined that no fluid could be seen moving through the opening. The major discrepancy was the fact that I didn't show the physical signs of someone with a closed or partially obstructed portal. I was coherent and clearheaded, and the majority of my pain was localized at the wound sites. I didn't feel excessive head pressure or dizziness. Dr. A explained that he had to put more faith in my individual sense of health because it was possible that the opening was just not visible on the scan. To my disappointment, I was kept at the hospital overnight for more observation.

I tried to take my mind off the news and maintain some degree of positivity, but it wasn't easy. I had fully anticipated leaving, and now I had the added stress of not getting any definitive prognosis. Mom and I tried to take a painfully slow walk around the floor, but I was too lightheaded from the extended time spent in bed to continue.

After eating and resting for a while, we thought it might be nice to go up to the roof to watch some fireworks. It was Fourth of July, and we had a pretty spectacular view of Manhattan. We tried to make the most of an unfortunate situation, so getting some fresh night air seemed like a good plan. It turned out to be a major disappointment and a sad memory marker I doubt I'll ever be able to erase.

I couldn't focus on the fireworks or appreciate the beautifully lit sky over the East River. I stood out on that roof, watching the small crowd of innocent IV-toting children stare into the night with a muddled mix of hope and desperation. There were patients in much worse shape, and I felt an overwhelming sadness for our respective circumstances.

Sadness bled into anger, and anger into despair. Is that what my life had become? Was I destined to forever be one of "the sick"? I thought I had found an answer to silence the worries and fears, but now I was standing on a roof during Fourth of July fireworks in Manhattan with a head full of worry and fear. None of us deserved that. We were children. We were blameless. We didn't believe our innocence would be stolen from us. It wasn't fair. It wasn't right. It wasn't a deck anyone should be dealt.

My head traveled to memories of the year before and the heavily attended outdoor event held at a local park near my town. I sat on that hill, watching the extravagant sky, contemplating the uncertainty of my freshman fall. A year later, with prior plans to be down at the shore with my college friends, I'd been delivered very opposite circumstances.

We went back to the room, and I did my best to find some perspective. It's incredibly tough to locate the light when you're deep in the tunnel. But even then, there was some small part of me that held tightly to hope. Maybe it was the ignorance of youth, but I couldn't fully invest in the notion that this was the only road I would travel. Feeling disappointment and frustration is not hopelessness. They are critically different emotions, and that dissimilarity is what separates those who survive from those who succumb.

The next afternoon, a doctor with a thick Austrian accent, who we incorrectly labeled as "Dr. Germany," removed the drainage catheter. The painful pulling caused an unusual sensation from the interior of my brain. I had generally experienced pressure originating from areas surrounding my ventricles. But this was unique. Because the catheter was inside my skull to regulate drainage, I could feel its removal. So after two neurosurgeries, I finally became intimately acquainted with the nerve endings in my command center. I wanted to offer my apologies for the recent intrusions, but they seemed pretty necessary. If it could speak, I'm sure my brain would agree.

Keish and her close friend returned for another visit. They had been there each day, supplying food, videos, magazines, games, and a change of clothes so Mom could take a shower and finally feel clean. They were an incredibly helpful distraction, skillfully taking my mind out of the hospital and back to happier spaces. Keish was a reminder of what I had and a motivator for what I could find again. She loved me. Bandages, scars, and bad haircuts never changed that.

The following morning, Dr. Germany returned with another resident to discuss my situation. He wanted to be sure the wound site from the catheter was sealed properly and that I had maintained my CSF levels during the night without the aid of additional drainage. All lights were green for discharge.

A couple of hours later, Dr. A arrived to answer all of our questions and concerns and gave the necessary instructions for the remainder of my recovery. He said we should return to his office for the staple removal and schedule a follow-up during my fall break from Ithaca. He was attentive and reassuring, and we had no reason to think he had trepidations of any kind.

We called Keish to take us home, and I began the emotional seesaw of desperately wanting to return to normalcy while simultaneously fearing the loss of my hospital security blanket. It was even more heightened this time, knowing that the chances of malfunctions and problems were no longer remote but real. The hope of a new life helped lessen the fear, but I wasn't feeling incredibly healthy, so the panic was more pronounced.

It was great to be back, and I was desperate to take care of the smallest personal details. Shaving, washing my hair, and clipping my nails were on the top of my list. It's shocking how crucial the little comforts in life can feel when they're taken away. I'm relatively high-maintenance, out of the gate, so a long stretch in the hospital makes it even more difficult to get comfortable. I savored the hot shower and the freedom to move on my own clock.

I started doing light normal activities over the next few days without significant problems. One irritating issue was my total inability to wear contact lenses. Any prolonged use caused splitting headaches behind the eyes. As soon as I took out the contacts, the headaches vanished. I assumed that the substantial decrease in intracranial pressure might have altered my prescription, so I wasn't overly alarmed. The surgical site was very close to the optic nerve, and that area can be sensitive to even the most minor modifications. Also, I was still lightheaded, but that could have been caused by my body's attempt to equilibrate the fluid levels.

I returned to the gym and relished my routine workouts. Being physically active had always been such an important part of my perception of health. My energy levels increased, and the psychological factor of seeing a fit form reflected in the mirror aided my progress immeasurably. The mind helped to heal the body. Oddly, the more strenuous the activity, the better I felt. Heavier weights and intensified running seemed to flush my fluids faster through the channels. This was the beginning of a pattern that repeated for years.

I finished the summer at home with Keish. I continued to improve each day, but I never found that elusive sense of perfect balance. The staples in my skull were removed, and Dr. A explained that I needed to be patient. My body and brain were used to relying on a pumping mechanism to perform a very necessary function. Now, they were working without ancillary help. It takes time to make that kind of transition. But I finally registered some level of success. I was back. I was cured. I was Pinocchio without the strings. We scheduled my follow-up, and he wished me luck in Ithaca.

THE UNRAVELING

I BEGAN MY journey in Ithaca as a young man with a manageable, albeit unsettling, condition. Now, for the first time in more than four years, I was back on a level playing field. There was a strong sense of relief, mixed with anxious anticipation. The pangs of my transition were still raw, but I was more than ready to leave behind the shadows of my past and live in the light for a while.

My "rebirth" was difficult to accept. I found myself frequently running fingers along my neckline and down my rib cage, almost unable to believe the shunt was gone. The physical benefits, including complete freedom of movement, were true gifts. But the lingering dizziness and occasional floating sensations were disconcerting. I justified any undesired effects by making excuses about stress, lack of sleep, etc. Creating hypotheses to explain the unexplainable was second nature.

One point that had been hammered home harder than anything else was how incredibly sick and dysfunctional my body would become if the newly created pathway closed. Since I was in decent working condition, I thought I could simply push through the discomfort and wait for better health. Sometimes the dizziness got worse, and that made sitting through long lectures challenging. But I tried to relax, reduce my stress, and take better care of myself.

Then, in the middle of October, I headed home for my fall break and my follow-up with Dr. A. Apprehension and concern paved the way to his office, but I was eager for some consoling news. I lay on that MRI table, overflowing with thoughts. The familiar rattling of the magnets distracted my daze, and the scan began.

It was not good news. The new films revealed an increase in the size of my ventricle since July. Dr. A reiterated that the current state of my health was a more accurate gauge of the procedure's effectiveness. I explained my symptoms, but even I didn't believe the words coming out of my mouth. I said that I had been experiencing some dizziness and headaches, but I was adamant about them not being the "bad headaches." This was partly true, but it was more because I had been accustomed to living life with a shunt system. These were new sensations, new rules.

Mom was upset and unsettled. She wished I had been more direct with the doctor about my feelings, but I thought I'd described the situation to the best of my ability. I wasn't a complainer, so I didn't really know how to judge the severity of my suffering. What might have seemed minor to me could have been a critical warning sign for someone else. A specific kind of pain means nothing and everything all at the same time.

My physical world had changed. There were a number of variables at play, and it was impossible to make clear delineations. This was unfamiliar territory for me, but the results of the scan didn't lie. I was back in the "unknown zone," and my time at home was anything but relaxing. The mental and psychological strain of these procedures far outweighed the physical damage. I did my best to take advantage of the week with old friends and drove back to school with an impressive weight on my shoulders. In less than a month, the other shoe fell.

I had secured a single room my sophomore year. A core group of friends lived together in a suite on campus, but I knew the constant activity and distractions would make it difficult for me to focus on my studies. I had the best of both worlds. I was able to socialize with them and still retreat to the sanctity of my own space when it was time to concentrate. The downside, I learned, is that my solitary living situation left me terribly vulnerable.

After eating lunch in the dining hall with my friend Eric, I noticed that the dull headache I woke up with that morning had gotten much worse. I told him I might go back to my room to lie down for a while. Because he had never seen me go anywhere near a nap, this plan sounded bizarre. But he told me to call him when I was ready for dinner and the gym, and we went our separate ways. What followed were the most confusing, desperate, and dangerous moments of my life.

I stood by the side of my bed contemplating my next move. It seemed ridiculous to lie down at that hour, but the pounding was getting exponentially worse, and I thought that sleep might be my only escape. There were a handful of situations when simply lying flat and motionless for an hour or two could alleviate a bothersome headache. I didn't have a surplus of options, so I went with my gut.

I called Mom to let her know the situation. The headache and dizziness were accompanied by an overall body ache, and she said that I sounded disoriented. She agreed that some peace and quiet was a good idea and told me she would call back to touch base. I called her ten minutes later. This was code red. I needed some serious help.

The next few hours were a mix of hallucinations, visions, and some almost indescribable examples of my body's ferocious will to stay alive. I couldn't believe how quickly the situation turned lethal. I can only remember flashes of images and thoughts. But I know I devised mini "survival plans," including forcing my whole hand down my throat to induce vomiting. This offered temporary relief until the small dorm garbage can was filled only with green bile. I had no idea what I was doing. I became an animal, scratching and clawing for the chance to take another breath.

One of the most remarkable symptoms of this fiasco was the return of what I called "supersonic hearing." There were flashes of this in my eighth-grade homeroom during that very first attack. I don't know what the brain does to summon this ability, but I could hear intelligible conversations from people in the student center, which was clear across campus. The voices in the hallway outside my door were thunderous and deafening. The fact that the body has this (normally untapped) potential power is mind-boggling. There is still so much left to learn about our anatomy.

Survival instinct is a mystery. There was a moment in that room where I couldn't figure out how to operate my desk lamp. I pushed it and shook it but never managed to press a simple button located plainly on the base. However, at one point, I dialed a sixteen-digit access code and phone number combination to call out for help. The "survival brain" took control of my hands. But the faint, trailing voice left on my home answering machine was haunting. It was the sound of a human being on his very last leg, close to collapse. In a tiny distant whisper I pleaded, "Mom. Please come. Thank you."

In the time between receiving a speeding ticket and arriving in Ithaca, Mom had called my aunt Jill, who lived in Upstate New York. She thought there was a chance Jill could get to me sooner, so she asked her to try. Jill then made a very strategic move that, quite possibly, saved my life. She called the campus police, notifying them of the situation. They responded immediately.

I floated in and out of a state of semi-consciousness. There were times when I could feel myself slipping away. People talk about seeing bright white lights or experiencing an overwhelming sense of calm. I believe I was on the precipice of life and death. My body was finally ready to concede defeat. I was out of fight, and I was out of time. Surprisingly, there was very little panic. The machine that strives so resolutely to live is also highly capable of easing the transition to surrender. It serves as warrior and protector, and I was lulled into a slow, steady darkness. Then, a sudden loud pounding shook me back to life.

I stumbled to the door, trying desperately to manipulate the locks and was greeted by two uniformed men. They told me they were with the campus police, but I could only see melting, liquefied shapes where their faces were supposed to be. I had a vague understanding that they were there to help, but it was too exhausting trying to reconcile my internal world with reality.

They explained that they had come to take me to the health center. This life preserver somehow registered, and I started following them into the hallway. They stopped me and said, "Son, I think you may want to put on some pants." Good point. I stumbled into the closet and eventually managed to get a pair of jeans on my legs. It wasn't pretty. I'm sure they thought I was under the influence of some heavy hallucinogens.

The car ride was a blur, and it felt like I was transported to the health center magically. Mom arrived shortly after, so she was able to more clearly explain the situation to a reasonably confused staff. I was asked some simple questions to test my cognition, and I couldn't seem to find the answers. But even though I wasn't able to tell them where I lived or recall the president's name, when they asked what I was studying at Ithaca, I sat up in the bed and clearly stated, "I'm majoring in corporate communications, with a minor in advertising/public relations." Apparently, my curriculum was a heftier file in my hard drive.

I was transferred, by ambulance, to Cayuga Medical Center. This hospital was a real departure from the facilities in Manhattan, so I was apprehensive about allowing any "serious work" to be done. I understood I had to be stabilized, but I wanted to be back in New York for my revisions or procedures. This thinking couldn't have been more wrong.

Dr. L was the attending neurosurgeon at Cayuga, and he was more than happy to comply with our decisions and to help facilitate our requests. He determined that I was no longer in a critical state and that we had the time necessary to make the transfer arrangements. He assured us that Dr. A would be contacted and that I would, most likely, be heading back to Beth Israel the following day.

I was checked into a room and received an IV drip that helped reduce the buildup of fluid. That hazy cloud was still looming, but shortly before dawn, I started to regain some awareness of my surroundings. Because of the confusion, I asked several questions about my situation and actually felt a little better. The headache and dizziness were still there, but reality was slowly returning. It was kind of like wiping a streak of water from a pair of glasses and finding some clarity. But that also meant a fresh head for worry.

Early in the morning, I had to get an MRI because the one CT machine wasn't working. It was hard to believe that any facility would have only one available scanner, but this was not the big city. At that time, this only fueled my stubborn eagerness to return to Manhattan. I was thankful to be stable, but I needed to get back to what felt familiar. My blinders were securely fastened.

The waiting game was tough. Dr. L was in surgery all day, so we had no contact with him until the evening. When he finally called, the information was uneventful. There was very little change in my scans, and another call had been placed to Dr. A to obtain his operative and pathology reports from my last procedure. There was even talk of having me transported to Beth Israel by ambulance or helicopter, but we waited for official word from Dr. A.

My friends from Ithaca stopped by for a visit, and my spirits improved. I know that the medication was a definite factor in my moments of clarity, but a nurtured soul can do the job just as well. Mom was back at my dorm gathering some things for the trip, so it was nice to have that time alone with them. Eric, Jay, Chris, and Sal pulled my focus away from that single monotonous track and back toward the hope of where I could return. Their concern was authentic, and they didn't need to do anything more than just be there. That's the beauty of sincerity. It takes so little effort.

Before Mom left, she wanted some help making a list of any items I needed from my dorm. I'm sure she expected the standard articles like pants, shirts, sweaters, specific books, etc. Instead, she got a painstakingly neurotic description of exactly which CDs should be taken, where they were located, how they were catalogued, and precise instructions about the way they were to be handled and transported. This preceded the days of MP3-packed digital libraries backed up on multiple external hard drives.

I maintained a flawless compact disc collection and treated my music like fragile crystal. There were thousands of scratch-free classics in multiple wallets, organized by artist and genre. Every lyric book and piece of artwork accompanied every album, and I knew each one like some member of a musical family. I was a passionate collector and an obsessive fan. Not much has changed.

Friday the 13th. One of my medications was stopped to see how I tolerated the change. The latest news was that I might not need to be transported as urgently as originally thought. We tried to confirm this through multiple calls to Dr. A, but he was a difficult man to reach. Neurosurgery doesn't allow for ample free time, but for those of us hanging on a string, the silence was a hard thing to accept. Frustrated and anxious, Mom made direct contact with his office and managed to catch him between rounds.

The worst possible news. Dr. A felt, after consulting with Dr. L, that I should be reshunted. I had demonstrated a history of "moderate success" with shunting, and the recent situation proved that my body could not sustain the benefits of a third ventriculostomy. This was the most medically sound decision. It was safe and logical, and it ripped the heart from my chest.

This realization spawned my first breakdown. The vivid recollections from my post-op shunt recovery, the agony of enduring that prison of immobility, and the seemingly endless road to physical recuperation struck me like a thunderous uppercut. I was normal again. I was healed. I was finished with the worry and pain and doubt. Why the hell would I want all of it back? System overload.

Through defiant tears, I explained to Mom that this was not going to be my life. They were not putting that synthetic snake back inside of me. I was taking my chances as a freethinking, untethered human, and I would rather die than begin the shunting nightmare again. I was adamant. I was steadfast. My will was broken, and Mom was crushed. This was my big moment. My last stand. But I hadn't even left the chair.

Ultimately, I decided to make the sacrifice for the benefit of everyone else. Letting the intracranial pressure build and allowing this affliction to end my life was selfish and irrational. It was prolonged suicide. I believed I had exhausted all the fight in my reserves, but that determination was impulsive and it came more from a place of fear than rationality.

The details of my discharge had morphed so drastically that the original idea of a helicopter or ambulance transporting me to Manhattan had disappeared. The low-dose steroid I was taking regulated my fluid levels so any symptoms remained dormant. As long as I stayed on that medication, there was no reason I couldn't drive home for the weekend and head to Beth Israel on Monday morning.

This was welcome news. I think Mom and I desperately needed a couple of recovery days before jumping into another hospital room. We went back to my dorm so I could take a final inventory, and I gathered anything I would need for the Thanksgiving recess. I stopped by the offices of my favorite English professor, Dr. V, to drop off a paper about prominent American writers of the 20th century. Even in the midst of a medical crisis, preparation was always at the forefront. That was probably a truer tale of how I felt and my faith in the future. There was forever some sense of better health waiting for me. I rarely did anything without a specific purpose. That was just my wiring.

The weekend was perfect. Mom was able to see Joyce and vent a little about her concerns. Keish came home from school for a couple of days for her cousin's birthday, so the timing was ideal. She was certainly anxious but remained unbendingly optimistic. We had some long talks and worked through the worry. When Keish, Mom, and I spent time together, the dark clouds on the horizon retreated for a while. That perception of safety was immensely comforting, and I'll never forget the relief I felt from the added oxygen.

The steroids, mixed with some psychosomatic positivity, kept the monsters at bay. Aside from some slight dizziness, I was fine. That was a troubling component of this affliction. Like my first procedure, I felt completely normal before going in for repair. The fluid balance is so delicate and a thin line separates disorientation and clarity. Unfortunately, this makes any eagerness for surgery pretty minimal. It's like loving your hairstyle the day you're supposed to have a haircut. There isn't much motivation for change.

Mom and I spent Sunday getting the house in order, organizing, and packing. It was odd to actually have time to prepare for this venture. Each preceding surgery began with such urgency there wasn't a second to think, let alone plan. Plus, the fact that I was almost back to normal made the trip to Beth Israel seem considerably less daunting. But we plodded along, collecting clothes, music, books, magazines, and our thoughts.

We left early Monday morning with Joyce. I had to be at the hospital by 10:00 a.m. for pre-op. After that, it was more of the waiting game. Medical facilities are like overloaded deli counters. The service is different, but the process is the same. We sat and talked and tried not to dwell on the inevitable. It was our third time down this road, so we were old pros.

At 2:30 p.m., I was taken to get my IV inserted and the old multiple puncture routine commenced. I dreaded this part. My nerves were raw, and I had the added pleasure of watching numerous needles miss their targets. I guess having thick skin is a blessing and a curse.

The surgery lasted about sixty minutes, and Dr. A reported that all had gone well. My head was not shaven, and smaller wounds and staples took the place of the multiple incision sites and generous stitching from the first shunt insertion. It was hard to believe how much the technique had evolved in such a short span of time.

I was told the recovery period would be a fraction of what I had to endure just six years earlier. There was no longer a need to lie flat in bed for all those days, my muscles wouldn't weaken as quickly, and the overall shock to my system was decreased due to the familiarity of the procedure. The brain sends specific signals to the healing mechanisms of the body when it recognizes the trauma. It's a form of muscle memory. I thought I had found a faint light in the tunnel. I was wrong.

It became very difficult to sleep. The staples in the back of my skull made the wound site sore and uncomfortable. My neck was constantly stiff as my body tried to manage the reintroduction of foreign matter to a space that was previously free. But the worst pain was from the small incision in my stomach. I could barely move without severe cramping. I explained the symptoms to Dr. A, and he said that because I had built a strong abdominal wall, there were more muscles to sever. He asked me to be patient and allow the body time to recover.

Turning on my side was impossible, and my ability to lift myself was diminished by the lack of abdominal strength. Basically, even though I was free to move, I couldn't. The only time I made it out of bed was when I was forced to go to the bathroom. I was compelled to stretch my muscles and bear the tearing sensations out of necessity. But these were more than routine healing pains. Something was definitely off, and there was no way I was going to be discharged without knowing exactly what that was.

The next day, I pushed myself to walk around, sit up in bed, and eat more regularly. My eyes were throbbing, and I found it too strenuous to focus on moving images, especially television. At first, I assumed it was more of the same eyestrain I'd experienced from past procedures, but the dull, throbbing headache, which started in the night, had carried over to the morning. All signs pointed to an error, but the question of *how* still remained.

Another day passed. I was supposed to be discharged, but my symptoms weren't getting any better. My uncle Pat was on his way to the city to take us home, but he only had a small window before he had to be back to pick up my cousins from school. We tried to keep him posted on the progress, but he made it all the way into Manhattan before we got the final word from Dr. A that I would not be leaving. I felt so bad, but Pat, always the consummate helper, didn't even flinch at the news. Dr. A thought that the fluid may have drained too quickly and the speed of that adjustment could have given me problems. He ordered another CT scan to verify that the amount of fluid in the ventricles had decreased. Unfortunately, the films weren't read in time to give Pat sufficient notice.

The scans didn't show the expected reduction in fluid levels, so a KUB X-ray was done to examine my kidneys, ureters, and bladder. The doctors wanted to see if there were any irregularities with the shunt itself. The results showed that the tubing was, in fact, coiled in my abdomen. It was similar to pinching a garden hose, stopping the flow of water in the middle. The fluid was leaving my brain, but was unable to empty into my abdomen. This disrupted the shunt's ability to regulate pressure levels and was the primary factor for my abdominal pain.

I was calm but annoyed. I felt this error was preventable and it was the second incident where Dr. A's "soft hands" did not penetrate something sufficiently. First, my third ventriculostomy opening closed because the membrane wasn't punctured thoroughly, and then he couldn't breach my abdominal wall to properly position the catheter. That was two strikes, and I wasn't hanging around for a third. The doctors waited to see if I could uncoil the tube myself. I waited to see if I could dampen my escalating frustration. Neither strategy yielded any results.

Another KUB was ordered. Nothing had changed. Surgery was scheduled. Again, no eating or drinking all day. My tolerance for discomfort was being tested, but the added challenge of fighting this irritation on an empty stomach pushed me to the brink. Whatever they were going to do, they needed to fix this problem once and for all.

The surgery was successful, and my tubing was uncoiled. Normally, this area was simple to penetrate, but the doctor needed to cut a wider space to establish the optimal insertion area. Dr. A blamed my unusually strong stomach muscles. I blamed his unusually weak fingers.

I was taken back to step-down, but I was slow to regain awareness. I had been through a lot, and I was a little tattered and torn. Dr. A mentioned that my body fought the anesthesia, a common reaction when two procedures are scheduled so close together. He referenced my tough abdominal wall and assured us the situation was resolved. Flow had been established, and he was confident there wouldn't be any further complications.

The hospital movie marathon continued. It seemed we were always in the recreation room selecting another video to help pass the time. It got to the point where we had movies running only to provide two-hour blocks of distraction. Often the films were turned down so low that Mom couldn't hear a word of dialogue. She never complained, never put her own needs above mine, and always kept vigilant watch at the foot of the bed like a member of the Royal Guard. Her stamina, tolerance, and patience were extraordinary. It's hard to explain how emotionally taxing a state of constant tension can be on someone. We lived in a world of relentless, sustained stress. Drugs put me to sleep. Mom didn't have that luxury.

I woke up very early, first at 4:30 a.m. and then at 6:00 a.m. The initial discovery was my lack of a headache. That perpetual dull throbbing was gone. Things were flowing again. But my stomach was a mess. Dr. A followed the same incision line, so the wound site was painfully tender. My abdominal muscles felt like they had been beaten with a sledgehammer, and the immobilizing cramping kept me glued to the mattress. I never realized how vital the stomach muscles were for movement. Sitting up was out of the question, and rolling onto my side was torturous. It was the closest thing to paralysis I'd ever want to experience.

Keish called to say she was driving from her school in Connecticut to the hospital to bring us home. It would take her at least two hours to make it into the city, so I had some time to figure out how to move and, more importantly, to think. I managed to get myself in a seated position, ate a small lunch, and watched some videos. I was pretty exhausted from the restless night, but I was more than ready to return to Newburgh.

My mind wandered. This had to be it. This had to work. The shunt was situated. The valve was in place. This should at least buy me some time. I could get back to school and back to life. I needed a break from being broken.

THE COLLAPSE

THANKSGIVING WAS SPENT in a state of cautious optimism. I was surprised by a visit from some of my Ithaca friends, who stopped by the house to drop off a gift. Eric, Jona, Jay, and the majority of my core crew wrote, shot, and edited a "get well" video for me. It was complete with interviews, skits, and some archival footage of times we spent together earlier that year. I couldn't believe it. They all had the pressure of midterm exams sitting on their shoulders, but somehow, they still found the time to get together to work on something they knew would brighten my spirits. Those were the kind of friends I had. I watched that tape so often I thought it would snap.

I was thrilled to be out of the hospital, but I was thrown right back into a fluctuating state of self-assuredness and doubt. I returned to the daily guessing game, questioning every ache or pain, and I was acutely aware of the familiar intruder inhabiting my skin. Because I have a hard time accepting situations beyond my control, this put me firmly back to square one. The only escape was to occupy my mind with practical distractions. My communications curriculum fit that bill nicely. So I went back to Ithaca, resolved and determined.

Less than a week later, I woke up in my dorm room with a soaked pillowcase. As I stood up, I looked down at my sheets utterly confused. I took a shower just before going to bed. My hair was damp but it was short. It didn't seem possible that the pillow could be this wet so many hours later. But to a semi-conscious morning brain, this seemed like a logical conclusion. I stumbled down the hall to hit the showers and get ready for class.

I opened the stall door in our communal bathroom to take my morning pee, and I noticed a clear liquid dripping on the floor next to the toilet. It was rhythmic, like a leaking faucet. I looked up at the ceiling, and the dripping stopped. I looked back down to the toilet, and it started again. This was the second time that morning I was baffled, and that was two times too many for that hour.

I stared at the ceiling, attempting to solve the riddle. Someone must have left a sink running or overloaded a washing machine. Yeah. That was it. Simple. There was some malfunctioning washer causing water to drip from the floor above. College kids can be so irresponsible sometimes. Why wouldn't they have contacted maintenance? This was the last thing I needed to deal with before a big quiz. Then I remembered I lived on the top floor.

The panic was immediate. I reached up to my head, and I realized that the clear liquid was coming from an exposed opening in my skull. Each time my eyes went toward the floor, a little more fluid dripped onto the tile. Somehow, my fresh head wound had opened during the night, and the excess CSF had found its own escape route. I thought about the risks of infection, sustained injury, or worse. I didn't know what this meant, but I knew it was serious. My mind raced. I was flooded with lists of unfinished business, plans to prepare, and a general circuit overload. Nothing else mattered. Life was on pause and fast-forward at the same time. I needed to figure out what to do, and I needed to figure it out fast.

Then, this calm wave settled over me. I still can't explain it, but I found myself quickly and efficiently formulating my exit strategy. I went back to my room, grabbed my shaving kit, and methodically shaved my face and neck. I clipped my nails and took an inventory of my things. If I was going back to the frontline, I was going there ready for battle. The little things make all the difference. Always the little things.

I took a bag of books and magazines, threw on a Yankees cap, and walked down to the health center. I never wear hats, but I thought the sight of someone strolling through campus leaking brain fluid might be alarming. Apparently, I was mistaken.

When I got to the center, I walked briskly past the rows of coughing seated students and up to the reception desk. I was told to write my name on a list using a pen attached to a chain. Evidently, pen theft was a legitimate concern. I explained that I had recently undergone brain surgery, a wound in my head had opened during the night, and I was leaking cerebrospinal fluid into my baseball hat. The woman at the desk paused for a beat, looked me in the eyes, and said, "Okay, I'm going to need you to go ahead and write your name on this list and have a seat. We'll call you when we're ready." I guess maintaining protocol was of supreme importance. So I took my place among the waiting crowd of winter colds, thoroughly shocked by the brazen dismissal.

Luckily, the medical staff behind the desk was a complete contrast. They understood the balance between being friendly and being efficient. I was treated with the care and urgency that my predicament required. Dr. L was called from a medical conference in Ohio, and he agreed to remedy the situation the following day if that was what we wanted. I was more than done with the blunders and miscalculations of Dr. A. Three strikes. He's out.

Another check-in, another hospital room. My bandages were changed every hour to help keep the opening clean and free of any infection. I was immediately NPO (*nil per os*), or nothing by mouth, so I ate everything I could until midnight. Patients are normally NPO before a scheduled surgery or even the possibility of a procedure. The stomach has to be relatively empty to prevent complications in the operating room. I'd been down that road before, so I knew I had to stock up while I had the chance. Any delays the following day would leave me starving. I filled the tank as much as possible.

Dr. L had two surgeries before mine, so I went through a battery of CT scans and X-rays to determine whether or not there was any issue with the tubing itself. They found no breakage or abnormalities of any kind. This was a minor relief because the implementation of new catheters had never been too kind on my body. The focus was exclusively on the valve. Dr. L needed to figure out what happened, why it malfunctioned, and how to prevent any future mishaps. It was a tall order, but I assumed things couldn't get any worse. A new set of eyes and hands was exactly what I needed.

Then, I waited. I spoke to some of my Ithaca friends, listened to my music, and seesawed between feelings of extreme positivity and utter despair. I could exhibit this great resolution and a general "out of my hands" philosophy as quickly as I could let my head go to the darkest places. My obsessive-compulsive demons ran wild with thoughts of death, a future tethered to a hospital bed, and any number of scary scenarios. My dichotomous nature had always been the central character in my story. As soon as my right hand grabbed for the next rung on the ladder, my left hand pulled it away.

In the late afternoon, I was prepped for surgery. Every facility is slightly different. At Cayuga, a "calming" medication is administered through the IV to help patients relax before a procedure. Well, it worked. This stuff was some type of pharmaceutical opiate, and I felt like I was floating 8 inches above the gurney on the trip from my room to the OR. I asked what I had flowing through my body, and one nurse jokingly remarked, "If this drug were available on the street, it would be very popular." Understatement of the century.

Mom walked across psychological hot coals, stuck in the waiting game once again. She spent over an hour lost in her head, hoping for the best and praying that this ordeal could finally be over. We both confronted each procedure with a mix of hopefulness and apprehension. We'd been burned before, but Dr. L had a sensitive, reassuring nature and we trusted him. Still, every brain surgery is a frightening experience. This time, I was whacked out of my mind on "hospital heroin," so the weight of the worry landed squarely on Mom's shoulders.

Out of surgery. There was a small blockage found near the valve's opening that compromised the flow. Dr. L replaced the valve with a similar unit. I always had slower CSF circulation, so he used a Delta, which was another low-pressure model. Dr. L also briefly mentioned newer valves that could be adjusted to handle varying degrees of pressure. There were regularly advancements in the field, and this was simply another. But he was confident the newly replaced Delta would solve my issues.

I was thrust back into recovery mode. My head hurt from the incision, and I was more tired than usual. I assumed this was because my body had been through the wringer, and I believed it was just a matter of time before I felt better. I ate what I could and tried to push through the night.

I woke up in the early hours of the morning with a bad headache. I usually tried to stay away from pain medication, but Mom finally convinced me to take something. I was given codeine for the second time and was instantly nauseous. From that point on, I listed codeine as a medication allergy. My stomach just couldn't tolerate it. More blood was drawn, and when the headaches got more severe, I was taken down to radiology for another CT scan. I began to experience the familiar "disconnected" sensations that accompany malfunctions. It seemed unthinkable, but something was definitely wrong. A call was placed to Dr. L.

The headache continued to intensify, and I felt even worse than the day before. Sleeping, as always, was my only respite. It's odd. Even though I sleep so little now, for a long time it was my only saving grace. There was something my head could do to heal itself when I was asleep that medication and cold compresses just couldn't match. Again, the body as a therapeutic machine is more intelligent and better equipped than we can fathom.

Eric and Jona came by for a visit. I masked my distress and did my best to be a good host. Having them there did wonders for me mentally, so forcing smiles through the pain was well worth the effort. Laughter really is the best medicine, and there were few people alive who could paint a brighter smile on my face than those two.

Dr. L responded to the page and sent instructions for me to be monitored. I vomited from the lengthy period of head pressure, shortly thereafter. The realization that I was only just beginning my hospital stay finally dawned on me. This was not a recovery/discharge situation anymore. We were definitely back to the drawing board. But with that news came a certain peace of mind. Leaving the hospital with my condition unresolved would have been far more unsettling. It was time to bear down and fix this lemon of a brain once and for all. Or die trying.

As usual, the severity of my symptoms seemed to change with the tides. Dr. L wanted to see if I could endure the discomfort until he figured out exactly what was wrong. Pain tolerance is one of my specialties, so I welcomed the challenge. He felt avoiding another quick revision would be in my best interest, and it would give him extra time to monitor and evaluate the situation. Sometimes these things can resolve themselves. This was not one of those times.

I was asked to journal every headache, any occurrence of dizziness or nausea, and to keep a record of what I commonly referred to as "the waves." These came to me in sudden bursts when I changed positions, abruptly sat up, or stood after lying in bed. Extreme pressure was followed by a moment of almost total blackness, and then my head and body found a way to recalibrate. They were scary and unpredictable. I hated the waves.

Dr. L came into my room to have a conversation while he examined the valve. He explained how difficult it was to pinpoint exactly what was causing my issues, but he had some ideas and wasn't going to give up the fight. I admired his resolve, and I found such comfort in his bedside manner. Then, he tested my valve by depressing the flushing chamber beneath the fresh incision and I nearly rocketed out of the bed. It was one of the most intense, explosive pains I'd felt and my body's natural reaction was to escape. He apologized, finished our talk, and left for the night. I then proceeded to have an unmitigated emotional meltdown.

As strong and resilient as I attempted to be, there were instances when I couldn't choke down, suppress, or stifle the heartache. This was one of those nights. I felt helpless, hopeless, and lost. I vented and sobbed, and Mom was there to offer her usual supportive ear and consoling words of encouragement. It was one of the most cripplingly sad moments of my life. But it was never the actual moment. It was the culmination of a thousand tiny cracks in the concrete, finally splitting the dam to set the water free. Thankfully, the sob session put me right to sleep.

Dr. L and his associates were on the case. They requested that all prior medical records and reports be sent to Cayuga. They also asked that I try to be as active as possible. This meant sitting up, moving, and walking around the halls. The doctors explained that they might be able to gauge my body's reaction to fluctuations in pressure if I actually compelled it to accommodate my changing positions. This proved easier in theory than in practice.

I'm a fighter, and I wanted so badly to force myself to get better. But I just couldn't beat the beast. Walking the halls was horrendous. Every few feet, I was hit with waves so harsh they knocked me up against the nearest wall. I gripped the concrete and waited for the rushes to subside, but it was a draining dance. I couldn't make it very far without getting smacked by another surge. My body ached. I got weaker by the minute. Frustrated, I headed back to the room feeling defeated. I tried to eat and get some recovery sleep. It was pretty obvious this was going to be more difficult than I thought. My hope was that Dr. L would find a definitive solution to this mess before the blizzard buried me.

Another serious concern was the completion of my coursework for the semester. At that point, I was undoubtedly missing my finals, and my major put a heavy emphasis on presentations. I was a diligent student, and the thought of not being able to finish my courses killed me. It was bad enough lying in that hospital bed, drowning in thoughts of my unpredictable future. I certainly didn't want the added strain of repeating a semester. Thankfully, my professors were also miracle workers.

I was never someone who skipped class or fell asleep on my desk. I relished the opportunity to learn new information, and I excelled in the classroom environment. Of course, papers and exams stressed me out as much as anyone else, but the interaction in a room between students and instructors was a process I enjoyed. Unbeknownst to me, this natural enthusiasm did not go unrecognized, and it ultimately paid off in spades.

When the news spread about my situation, my professors snapped to action. I received visits, phone calls, cards, and gift baskets. The outpouring of support was remarkable. They explained that they would be making concessions and offering alternate assignments in place of any presentations or group meetings I missed. I was floored by their compassion, and I vowed never to squander second chances.

Gripping my shoulder harness and waiting for the ride to end is the only way I can describe that week. IVs were changed, veins were blown, and the head pressure continued to build. Sitting, moving, and walking were nearly impossible, and I was on the frayed end of my tolerance. I can play the waiting game better than most, but chasing racing doctors and endless empty hours stuck in bed is a recipe for agitation. It was prison, with better sheets.

Feeling like I couldn't take much more, I got a visit from Dr. L that lifted the needle from a skipping record. After monitoring my case and weighing the possible options, he decided that my fundamental issues were pressure related. My shunt malfunctions, especially the most recent, were due to a combination of debris buildup and the lack of force needed to flush that debris through the chamber. He recommended the implantation of a programmable valve.

This unit used a regulation system built on magnets, and the adjustments in pressure could be made without surgery. Also, the structure of this valve allowed larger debris to pass through more easily. It sounded like the perfect solution, and we weren't exactly drowning in options.

Dr. L had recently undergone the training necessary for this procedure, so I would be his first case. Part of me was concerned with my role as the guinea pig, but I knew that he would be even more careful and attentive navigating uncharted territory. Plus, I believed he wanted this to work for me. He had been extremely sympathetic during my ordeal, and I thought it would bring him personal satisfaction to play a part in my healing.

So my fifth brain surgery was scheduled, and I went back into mental prep mode. It was never easy to ready myself for the inevitable, and I often let my mind slip into dark places. This was my fourth neurosurgery in five months, and it was hard not to wonder about my body's tolerance and limitations. Granted, I was only nineteen years old. But even the freshest bodies can have trouble when subjected to that many invasive procedures. As always, I took stock of the situation and had a calm, matter-of-fact discussion with Mom about the potential troubles that could arise from another session under the knife.

It was disturbing for her to hear me say those things, but I needed to communicate my wishes clearly and without emotional filters. I gave her specific instructions about organ donation, avoiding extraordinary measures to keep me alive, and cremation. I stated my plea for her to continue her life without me and to use my case to help bring education and awareness to others. It was a somber and pragmatic speech, but those things had to be said. It was a moment of clarity, and it would be impossible to express myself after the fact.

Luckily, I lived to babble another day. The surgery was a success. However, my postoperative experience was unusually difficult. I got very upset in recovery, and the decision was made not to allow Mom in to see me. In the ICU, I was still sad and noncommunicative. I looked like I'd been smashed by a train, and for some reason, when Mom tried to talk to me, I dismissed her with a wave of my hand. I hadn't experienced any of those emotions after previous surgeries, but the brain is mysterious. It's impossible to gauge what effect that kind of trauma has on the subconscious or what residual memories are brought back from the anesthetic adventure. Either way, I was not myself.

Strangely, the next time I had any awareness of my surroundings, I had no memory of my post-op experience. At one point in the night, I had even requested that I be catheterized when I wasn't able to pee. As soon as the nurse began to insert the tube, I felt a burning sensation and immediately asked her to remove it. All night, I had moments of confusion, discomfort, and restlessness. But it was dreamlike, and I was pretty shocked when I heard the details of my behavior the next morning. I had already been baffled by so much of what my brain had done throughout this ordeal. This was just another tally mark on the list.

My body did not snap back as fast as I had anticipated. I was generally a sluggish healer, but this time it felt like I couldn't even begin to find my rhythm. I was beaten and bruised, and my internal generator went into shutdown mode. Phone calls and day visits from my Ithaca crew were a huge help, but the nights were long. A bony ribcage and spindly arms replaced my gym-earned muscles. Constant congestion and nose bleeds from the hospital air made resting sporadic. Each day, I felt like I was getting weaker and heading the wrong way down recovery road. I needed a change.

The machine to which I'd been tethered since the surgery was a squealing, beeping box from hell. I had a series of thin wires stretching from the front of the electronic unit to the inside of my head. On the LCD, a flurry of digital peaks and valleys monitored my movements and pressure changes to help the doctors ascertain my ideal valve settings. But the fun didn't stop there. If I shifted, even the slightest bit, a high-pitched alarm signaled the change in my intracranial pressure levels. This made rolling over on my side during the night feel like something out of a James Bond film. I used a series of intricate, orchestrated movements to put myself in a defensive crouch. Then, with one squinted eye on the monitor, I applied some trapeze artistry to adjust my position without waking the digital sleeping giant. It was my own little insomnia game, endless and exhausting.

However, the overall results were positive. From a neurological standpoint, Dr. L was thrilled with my progress. The pressure headaches were completely gone, and those dreaded waves hadn't hit my shore since the procedure. He was confident there would be no threat of a malfunction, and he was pleased with the functionality of the new valve. This was the outcome he wanted, and his general demeanor grew even more calm and reassuring.

Mom was such a trooper. She filled the limitless hours with constant food runs, video rentals, trips back to the college for my mail, and diligent communication with the doctors and nursing staff. Having that weight taken off my shoulders was invaluable. I could let someone else handle the business while I focused on recuperation. She was astoundingly selfless and patient. I don't know how she kept her sanity. Like Andre Agassi, she's a Zen master.

Eventually, the intracranial monitor was removed, and the external drainage tube was detached. Fighting fatigue, I tried to be as active as possible. I was still dizzy and congested, but each day brought steady progress and a renewed spirit. A return to normalcy was approaching, and I had a feeling I might be exiting the woods shortly.

On December 15th, we got the news I would be discharged. As always, panic accompanied relief, but I was thrilled I was going to be able to spend Christmas at home. This was a long battle, and it was time to savor some peace after the war. I desperately needed my own bed and a small sliver of familiarity.

I was sent home with all my CT scans and the two operative reports. At this point, I'd built myself a nice collection of surgery-related souvenirs. Every time I checked out of a hospital, I thought I would look back at that particular struggle as being my last. I assumed that all that pain would be a distant memory, only marked by some arbitrary anniversary date, signifying my final procedure. Thinking any other way would be counterproductive to my healing, but it was impossible not to wonder if another fire was waiting to burn.

I arranged a gathering of my friends at Ithaca before we went back downstate, but the imminent reality of the outside world was overwhelming. Just before we left, I struggled trying to get a Yankees hat over my fresh wounds. No matter how I manipulated its placement, the buckle rubbed against my scalp. Standing in the bathroom, taking stock of the futility of the situation, I opened the floodgates.

It was too much to handle. The culmination of such extreme levels of physical and emotional stress had gotten the better of me, and I couldn't hold back. I looked into that mirror and saw a withered, broken shell. My former self had disappeared, and what remained was a feeble depiction of that person. I stared more deeply, trying to see where that confident, enthusiastic smile had gone. I looked for a small spark behind the eyes or some flash of life. Hollow emptiness was all that stared back. It was the frightening revelation of how far I'd fallen.

I was angry at myself for thinking I could be the man I was. I hated this condition, and the lies and hopes that came with it. Leaving the hospital would only put me back into the world of the normal. I was anything but normal. I didn't belong there anymore, and it seemed senseless to pretend that I did. Tears of frustration and self-pity soaked my face. It was one of the lowest points of my life. Still, I tossed the hat in a bag, and with scars exposed, I made my way to campus.

Walking into the communal suite shared by a group of my friends felt both soothingly familiar and sadly foreign. Everyone was in the throes of finals week, and a steady stream of visitors buzzed in and out to say hello. I sat on the couch and watched people go through the motions of normal collegiate life. Even though I had been unplugged from the mainframe for only twelve days, I felt so different, so disconnected.

It's remarkable how quickly one can gain perspective. I shared their worried faces, stressed muscles, and furrowed brows. I sacrificed sleep for study sessions. I woke up so nervous before presentations that I threw up in the shower. I heard the incessant knocking of the future at my door. Everything we did was to assuage the pressure of expectations. I loved being a student. It was never about the grades. I appreciated the academic process. The report cards were for our families and prospective employers.

But I met a monster far meaner than finals and more terrifying than any lecture. I slayed the beast, or at least I put it to sleep for a while. Now, I just needed to remember how to return to a world that once felt like home. It was similar to slowly sliding into a hot tub. It takes some time to get acquainted with a system shock. With the semester already over and a mountain of work waiting for me, time was the last thing in my favor.

Being home was comforting, but I never let the dust settle. Even though I was given a full semester to complete everything I had missed, I decided I would finish all my required assignments before returning in January. I wanted to begin the winter on par with everyone else. Besides, I didn't need two semesters of work attacking me in tandem.

My professors clearly outlined what was required to complete my courses, and the alternative assignments were challenging but manageable. I read and wrote and worked until I got too tired or dizzy to continue. Communication classes put a heavy emphasis on group work and collaboration, so finishing all of this at home, alone, was an odd experience. Still, the crux of the material was there, and I felt I had grasped and absorbed as much as everyone else. I was fiercely determined to continue without lag. My ghastly scar and vacant self-esteem were big enough hurdles. The academic element was still controllable.

About a week before returning to Ithaca, we had an appointment with Dr. L. He was happy with my progress, and he tested the valve to be sure it was filling and releasing quickly. The wound sites were still very sore, so this wasn't much fun. But I knew he needed to trust the functionality of the system before he gave me a confident endorsement. I craved that more than anyone knew. So with lingering reservations and a dearth of excuses, I went back to school.

I returned that semester a very different version of myself. My confidence was depleted, and the easy smile was replaced by a wary grin. It became obvious how much stock I put in my physical appearance and how lost I felt without those tools at my disposal. It's something that can't be explained to outside observers. But watching the world from behind my eyes and seeing the criticism and pity returned made me feel a kind of hollowness I wouldn't wish on my worst enemy. Standing in line at the school bookstore with an armful of purchases while trying impossibly to hide the gaping wound and scar that spanned the back of my skull induced a degree of panic I will never forget. This was Blair 2.0. Downgraded.

College is as much about finding yourself as it is planning your future. The struggle for individuality and acceptance is just as demanding as a full course load. Hormones are raging. The line between adolescent hijinks and adult responsibility is blurred and then slowly erased as we ultimately unearth our true identities. Bearing the weight of the world, any added baggage can make for a Sisyphean climb.

Ithaca was an environment where I felt excited, accepted, and loved. My friends built the kind of support structure only found in idyllic films and starry-eyed fiction. But that's what we had. It was unconditional, and the bonds we formed were forever. That cushioned catapult was the only vehicle I could have used to rediscover my peak.

The pieces fell back into place slowly. There were still some scary headaches, but they were the healing kind. I was so gun-shy at that point; deciphering knee-jerk reactions from legitimate concerns was a problem. But I knew the more I thought about the worst, the faster the worst would find me. I needed to force away the thoughts of impending malfunctions and focus on the belief of true wellness. I had to trust the procedure. I had to listen to my body and have faith in myself. After five brain surgeries, I needed to understand that I was fixed. I had to find hope. Easier said than done.

THE LIFE BETWEEN

COLLEGE LIFE COMMENCED without missing a beat. Because I had finished all my previous semester's incompletes, I could comfortably share a seat on the same train with everyone else. People even remotely connected to me were well aware of my situation, so any feelings of isolation or insecurity were all my own. To the rest of the world, my bony frame and conspicuous wounds were invisible.

It was a little haunting returning to the dorm where life had so nearly faded away, but maintaining my single room was a necessity and I quickly fell back into a routine. There was plenty of work to be done, and that didn't include the preparations I still had to make for my internship in Los Angeles the following fall.

I healed a little bit more every day and found a way to use my hair to cover the scars. Unfortunately, wherever the surgeons drilled into the skull, they killed the nerve endings and follicles. This resulted in a head full of "dead zones" where I had very little sensation and slightly less hair growth. Fortunately, I was blessed with a thick mane, so these sites were normally undetectable. But I was more sensitive about the physical aspects than anyone else.

I returned to Newburgh that spring after my presentations and finals were finished. I worked for the Board of Education, mowing, mulching, and tending to properties in the school district. The grounds crew consisted of other college guys (and many of my friends from high school), so we had a blast. We worked outside, traveled from school to school with near-total autonomy, and socialized off the clock. It was a difficult gig to secure, but children of educators got a faster foot in the door. Being a night owl, I hated the early mornings, but I enjoyed the physicality and the camaraderie. I had some money in my account and the beaches of SoCal on my mind. The summer was a return to basics, and that comfort factor was exactly what I needed before I embarked on my trip out west.

Things with Keish started to cool by the spring of our sophomore year, but we still maintained regular contact. Her school was about five hours away, and she didn't stay in Newburgh that summer. We lived very different lives, but even with the distance, our connection was powerful. We transitioned into more of an open relationship, realistic about the importance of a full college experience. We didn't want to inhibit each other's growth or evolution. But whenever we came back together, the strength of our foundation was undeniable.

However, shortly before I was scheduled to begin my cross-country trip, she visited me in Newburgh and the gap seemed more severe. I knew I was about to take a significant step away from a road that felt familiar, and Keish was a crucial piece of that path, that past. At times, I let future prospects smother my present reality. The lure of my semester ahead blinded me to the importance of salvaging what little time we had together. This set in motion a pattern of inconsideration toward her that I deeply regret.

In the middle of August, I pulled out of my driveway in a Toyota Corolla stuffed with provisions for a life three thousand miles away. I was en route to Eric's house in southern New Jersey. We eventually attached our friend Brian to complete the convoy. Three cars, three drivers, no cell phones, and nothing but the open road lay ahead of us. Our levels of enthusiasm and apprehension were very different, but our destination the same.

For me, this was so much more than a semester in a cool new city. It was an affirmation that I was healthy and finally free. Every mile west was another mile away from the safety of my surgeons and the security of home. I had no doctors on standby and no plans of making any medical contacts in LA. Maybe it was foolish of me to be so ill-prepared, but I needed to feel the release of my shackles. My CT films were buried in the trunk, the only evidence of my secret Achilles' heel.

Eyes opened to a world I never could have conjured. I didn't do much traveling as a kid, so watching the country unfold before me was dreamlike. The space between the coasts was shocking. We're so accustomed to the speed of air travel that we forget how much land is out there. Driving for thirteen hours past an endless succession of Kansan sunflower fields is a pretty unmistakable reminder.

Armed with a few long-distance walkie-talkies as our only means of communication, the three of us stayed close enough to track. The radios had a short two-mile range, so we did our best not to drift. Eric was undoubtedly the navigator of our expedition. He possessed a preternatural ability to know exactly where he was in the world at all times. It was like an unflappable internal compass, and we followed him gladly. He was comfortable taking control, and this was not the first or the last time he would play the role of captain.

As his reward for piloting our caravan so proficiently, Eric was able to experience the terrifying panic of having a gun shoved in his face. It seemed like a random case of bad luck, but things got much worse for our fearless leader before we arrived in Burbank.

We stopped for dinner in Kansas City. Exhausted and overjoyed to be sitting down in a seat that wasn't moving, we ate, laughed, and yapped about our future lives in Los Angeles. It wasn't a bad spot or a bad part of town. The area seemed fairly commercial, and there was enough traffic not to feel isolated or nervous. Even though it was late, some families were still eating, and the parking lot was well lit.

These factors didn't seem to bother the men in the van that skidded up to our cars as we walked out of the restaurant. We went to our separate vehicles, and I noticed Eric talking to one of the guys crouching near the van. My gut said something was wrong. As I made my way over to him, the man jumped back into the van, the doors slammed shut, and it sped away. I asked Eric why he was talking to this stranger, but his wide eyes and clenched jaw told me it was time for us to get in our cars and disappear.

We drove until we reached our motel for the night, and then I got the full story. While Eric was unlocking his door, he turned to see a young thug with a gun pointed at his neck. The agitated kid wanted Eric's wallet and cash, but he was determined to make it quick. Eric maintained a cool head and convinced him that his credit cards had been canceled and that he only had a twenty-dollar bill. Instead of taking the time to argue, he snatched the twenty from his hand just as Brian made his way over to investigate. When he saw Brian, he jumped into the van and the driver sped away.

Eric was shaken, but it was more the surprise of the whole situation that sent his mind reeling. The juxtaposition between our happy dinner and a gunpoint robbery in less than five minutes was more than enough to throw him off balance. But his skilled acting and collected demeanor prevailed, and we had our first big tale of the trip. We figured that isolated incident was all the negative excitement the universe had in store for our trio. We were sorely mistaken.

My brain and camera were full of memories when we pulled into Vegas the night before our last push to LA. It was a time for celebration, a chance for us to reflect on the journey we'd taken, and a moment to anticipate the experiences waiting for us in our new home. It was also a perfect opportunity for Eric's passenger window to get shattered in the hotel's parking garage.

We got a call from hotel security informing us that one of our cars had been damaged. I was in the shower when Eric knocked on the door to give me the news. With pits in our stomachs, we walked downstairs to find out whose fate was sealed. Our intrepid skipper was handed another nasty slap from the universe.

Eric had a smaller, more packed car, and we assumed that the higher visibility level was to blame. So we sat in the security office and attempted to make some sense of the predicament. He tried to compile a list of the countless items in the vehicle, every few minutes recalling one more painful reminder of what had been taken from him. To exacerbate the situation, Eric and his mom had painstakingly purchased almost all the items for our shared kitchen. But there were already far too many insults on top of his pile of injury. That was just one more.

We left Vegas that afternoon trying to regain some semblance of enthusiasm for the last leg of our trip. Eric used a garbage bag and duct tape to "repair" the damage and had the added joy of listening to the wind whip through the gaps in his doorframe for more than four hours. Brian and I were clearly sympathetic, but we certainly felt lucky to have dodged a bullet.

About an hour outside of LA, we lost radio contact with Brian, so Eric and I pulled off the road and waited for him to catch up. We had a long talk about his state of mind and how he was planning to process the devastation. Eric, as always, gushed with coolheaded logic. He explained that he had already made his peace with the situation. He understood things would be more difficult for him in the beginning of our stay, but ultimately, everything that happened was for a reason. He had a way of compartmentalizing tragedy that floored me. Every single thing he owned was gone. Yet he was able to step outside of the situation to analyze things rationally. I would have been a shaking, crying mess all the way to Hollywood.

The apartment complex that Ithaca rented in LA was incredible. It was built around a sea of temporary housing units occupied primarily by actors, models, executives, students, and musicians. There was a fitness facility, two pools, rooftop tennis courts, hot tubs, a general store, and a clubhouse. But we could have pulled into an empty parking lot in the back of a dilapidated hostel and I still would have believed my life had changed for the better. The energy was palpable, and oddly, it felt like I was finally home. As someone born and raised an hour from Manhattan, the West Coast romance was unexpected. Still, it pulsed in my bones. This was love at first sight.

We spent the weekdays in class and at our various internships and our weekends soaking up the show business scene. I was able to lock down a gig in college radio promotions at a well-known independent record label. It was the quintessential LA job. Everyone was beyond relaxed, there was no enforced clock or dress code, and things still functioned smoothly. There is a misconception that Angelenos spend their days in board shorts, eating at outdoor cafes. That may well be the case in certain neighborhoods, but businesses are still run by businesspeople. You can't take a day off when the rest of the world is working. I think the residents of Los Angeles have just figured out a way to strike a better balance between the gifts and the grind.

The label welcomed me as an actual employee. I never felt like a lackey, and I was never treated with anything but respect. I scored a ton of free music, I was given creative autonomy when contacting music directors around the country, and I fell deeply for a fellow intern named Jenny. We lived on our own, went to grownup jobs, and did it all with the eagerness and ambition that propels the world of college kids. It was one of the happiest times of my life.

I kept a fairly hectic schedule, trading experiences for sleep, but I felt good. Occasionally, a slight headache would surface, but I could usually alleviate pressure by heading to the gym. Running and lifting weights caused any built-up fluid to drain more easily. Fortunately, I never reached a point where I felt overly nervous or in danger. So much of my physical health was dictated by psychological and emotional states. I was mentally healthy, and that translated into feeling good. But without a medical safety net in place, there was little room for concession.

Eric and I grew closer than ever. We shared the apartment with Brian, but often our idiosyncrasies (e.g., babbling incessantly about our hair products and taking two hours to leave the room) sent him looking for friends elsewhere. I'll admit, ours was a hard bond to break, and the inner circle was faithfully protected. We simply found ourselves on the same page. He was dating a young actress. I was with Jenny, my serendipitous mate from the record label. Eric and I walked very similar paths with a very similar style. It was a level of friendship that took me eighteen years to find, but it was clear that this person would be in my life for the long haul. Also, Eric was fully aware of my medical situation and kept a watchful eye for any irregular behavior on my part. The number of times he protected me or safeguarded my best interest is incalculable. Composed, understated, and sincere, he is the best friend anyone could ever have.

Our shenanigans in LA could fill volumes. Eric's close friend, Tim, on leave from his college in New Jersey, spent the end of the semester with us. He practically moved in and became an integral part of our team. He was a powerful addition to the group, and he assimilated easily into the LA lifestyle. Tim and Eric shared a long history from high school, and I certainly understood the connection. I first met Tim at the end of my freshman year at the shore house, and we forged an immediate bond. Tim completed our trio, and his presence added exponentially to the energy and spirit of the apartment. Every peg fell perfectly into place. I couldn't have written a better last lap.

December arrived, but leaving our happy West Coast lives proved more difficult than we anticipated. We watched our fellow Ithacans board planes or load cars for the drives back to their respective towns, but we pushed our stay to the very limit. Brian decided to head east with a different group, so for our trip home, Tim was in Eric's car and I was in mine. Traveling together made for a fitting final chapter.

Although I was thrilled to see Mom again, there was little else motivating me to leave. Abandoning 80° winters to be blasted by a frigid nor'easter felt insane. I missed Jenny instantly, and I couldn't deny that I was walking away from something powerful. We had some incredible times together, and to end a romance for no reason other than circumstantial factors felt unnatural. We both knew there was an inevitable finish line, but that didn't make the actuality of our separation any easier. Exit from paradise, heavy on the brakes.

The most notable detail of our trip home was my abrupt deviation from the plotted course before we even made it out of California. Looking back now, the situation seems comical. But at the time, circumstances reached a level of frantic intensity never before experienced by the Schuyler family.

Our walkie-talkies were a blessing and a curse. The fact that we could communicate during a time without cell phones was great. But the two-mile range limitations plagued us incessantly. Two miles seems like a reasonable distance, but when two cars are traveling at 70 miles per hour, that lifeline disappears pretty quickly.

Our main impediments were the large big rigs that dominated the landscape across most of Middle America. When there were no other vehicles on the road, semis, trailers, and other delivery trucks were the only moving objects for miles. Occasionally, these trucks would find their way between our two cars, and without a visual mark on Eric's Nissan, it was easy for me to fall behind. This was a consistent issue that irritated us on both legs of the trip.

On a stretch of desert, close to the California/Arizona border, this is precisely what happened. We were supposed to take an approaching exit. Eric radioed me with the instructions, and I watched him drift into the lane and take the turnoff. However, before I could follow, a semi slid next to me and attempted to pass me on the right. The timing could not have been more perfect if I had been part of a prank show, and the driver was specifically directed to make me miss my turn. I stared in shock as my car sailed past the off-ramp.

This was not an urban environment where exits pop up every few hundred feet, so I quickly veered toward the target and ended up on a road just behind the original intended mark. I drove frantically in Eric and Tim's direction. I had a rough idea of their trajectory, but I wasn't blessed with a keen sense of orientation, so it was basically blind hope.

After a few minutes of chasing them, I heard a faint static signal on my walkie-talkie. Then, Eric's voice blared from the minispeaker like some angel delivering a message. He tried to explain where they were and how I could get back to them. They drove toward me and waited for me to make contact. Eric gave me possible routes to take, and I desperately looked for signs to help correct my course.

Then, I lost it. I found the right road, but there was a construction detour that sent me on a loop in the opposite direction. The signal was dropping fast, so I decided to make an abrupt U-turn to get back to where I started. However, I didn't see the concrete divider separating the lanes, and I hit it at full speed.

My Corolla went airborne and smashed down onto the other side of the yellow lines. The boxes of dishes and other kitchen items that were packed neatly in cardboard boxes in my trunk collided with a crash. I was positive my tires were flat and my axle was destroyed. I screamed and swore into the walkie-talkie, and that was the last communication I had with them.

I pulled over to assess the damage. Miraculously, everything seemed to be fine. My tires were okay. The dishes had simply fallen on top of one another, with only a few broken. There didn't seem to be an issue with the axle or operation of the vehicle in any way. I couldn't believe it. That car was a tank. Still, I was on an unknown road in an unfamiliar part of the state. I had absolutely zero radio contact or any way to communicate with Eric and Tim. I was lost.

There are moments in life when we need to react to crises. People tend to handle these situations with varying degrees of success. Some shut down and shut off. Some panic. Some stop, breathe, and analyze. I am firmly in the camp of the latter. Maybe it's because I've had to deal with so much at such an early age, or maybe it's just my hardwiring. But colossal thorns have always hurt less than tiny splinters. It's counterintuitive, and it's another aspect of my personality that's inconsistent with conventional wisdom.

So I drove. I was shaken but calm. I knew I was well outside the limits of our radios, and there were only a few options available. I could pull over and wait for Tim and Eric to come into range. I could return to the original exit and hope they made the decision to circle back. Or I could assume they continued on the plotted course, and I could follow suit. The idea that this last notion seemed the most plausible is difficult to accept, but my brain said, "Keep driving, kid. You're on your own now."

Equipped with an unopened box of emergency road supplies in my trunk, I drove into the night. The plan was to keep moving until sleep became absolutely necessary. It was a day of delays, so I had to clock some extra hours to get back on schedule. That was never an issue. I found that driving in the dark was easier and more soothing. Besides, there was a lot to process. I used the quiet time to contemplate.

Naïve was probably the best way to describe my actions. When my body let me know it was time to rest, I found a motel and devised my attack plan. I used the maps from my emergency kit to chart my course back to Newburgh. It was probably the first time I ever forced myself to actually read and understand cartographic material of any kind. Normally, I spun in circles like a lost child in the mall if I made more than three turns outside my comfort zone. I highlighted the various interstates, located the transfer points, and went to sleep feeling confident in my decision to drive across America alone.

Knowing that Mom would view this new strategy quite differently, I decided a quick morning phone call was the best way to inform her that I was now a lone wolf. She was at work, so I was going to leave a reassuring message telling her I was safe and on my way to the next stop. I tried to collect myself and not let the nervousness come through in my voice. The phone rang for less than a second and I was greeted by a tribal, almost animalistic, howl. It came from the deepest recesses of the human spirit, and it was terrifying. I thought she was having a massive heart attack. Apparently, the cat fled the bag.

Mom was well aware of the events that transpired since I dropped communication with the guys. After circling the "area of last contact" for half the night, Eric made the decision to reach out to her, thinking that I might have called home to touch base. This set in motion a series of events and strategies that could rival the elaborate coordination of a government manhunt.

I learned that I was presumed kidnapped (even though I was twenty years old) and that a state investigation unit was using its resources in an attempt to pinpoint my location for retrieval. I never knew that Eric and Tim heard my crash and scream over the walkie-talkie or that they went back to look for my car. Understanding that I had zero ability to navigate, they assumed the worst when no car was found.

To think I continued driving across the desert was unfathomable to them. They spent a sleepless night at the motel contacting Mom at the recovery effort headquarters she established in Newburgh. My family had gathered. Tears were shed. The situation was on the verge of a vigil.

Confidence and excitement about my "mission" quickly turned to shame and regret. Reality landed. The ignorant thought process behind my scheme became cripplingly clear, and I felt terrible for having put my friends and family through that. I shaved some years off Mom's life that night, but I did so without the slightest clue. We talked for a while, and she slowly regained composure. She gave me Eric and Tim's phone number at the motel, and I called my friends to tell them I was still alive. It was time for a reunion.

I made my way back to where we started. There was a piece of me that was disappointed I wouldn't be able to complete the solo voyage. But the larger and more intelligent part of me realized how insanely foolish that would have been. Besides, this was another experience for us to share. I wanted to be with these guys, and if my disappearing act didn't top the list for the biggest story, we'd have to go build some more headlines together.

Thankfully, I can report that nothing else hit the same level of excitement for the rest of our trip. We tried to make the most of our adventure, but driving home is just never the same as driving away. Tim, Eric, and I were rarely at a loss for words or laughs. Unfortunately, the California sunshine was getting dimmer by the mile, and it was time to face reality. The sound of the alarm clock was rudely ending the dream.

But I can't say we were entirely devoid of drama. We took a largely southern route back, painting a trail across Texas and up the eastern coastline. It was mid-December, so we felt this was the best way to avoid inclement weather. Luckily, we managed to escape any winter storms or major blizzards.

Fully saturated with the South, we blew into Louisiana, ready to zipline back to the tri-state area. But the travel gods had one last slap in the face in store for us. To continue the blissful trend of car thievery, the valets at our hotel in the Big Easy stole our walkie-talkies.

I was exhausted from the previous leg, so I chose to stay in the room, call Jenny, and crash early. Tim and Eric wanted to hit the town and soak up a little bit of pre-Katrina New Orleans. Instead, I took a short walk to find some food, but several street dealers pushing coke and pills shortened my stroll. Regardless, I was beyond tired and had a heavy pit of longing in my stomach that food couldn't fix.

I barely heard Tim and Eric come back later that night. Had we been traveling to LA, I would have squeezed every last second of our time together and woken up alert and anxious to continue the trip. But this was a different journey, and my eagerness to dive into the social pool was waning with each passing day.

The three of us felt a collective letdown, but being closer to the East Coast invigorated us, and we were ready to go home. The valets delivered our cars, we tipped them well, and we headed down the street. Pretty quickly, we realized some very important items were missing from our vehicles. The walkie-talkies had been taken. Our lifelines, and only means of communication, were gone. We'd already experienced how difficult it was to maintain contact with these simple devices when I got separated. Now, we would feel what it was like to drive without them altogether. Thank you for bringing the cars around so quickly. Here's some money for stealing our stuff. This was not the jazzy sendoff we expected. We sped back to the hotel for some answers and a little justified ranting.

We spoke to the manager of the garage, and he was barely apologetic, almost expecting us to stamp his valets as thieves. At one point, he made a phone call explaining that this employee "had done it again." Nice to know we weren't his first victims. During a time of heavy layoffs and competitive employment, those valets had some pretty impressive job security.

Eric definitely didn't need a sticky hand in his pocket for the third time, but he absorbed and processed the situation as usual. Even with this small theft, I was furious. I couldn't imagine how he felt when everything he owned was taken. Luckily, we only had a short stretch ahead of us. In a couple of days, we'd be back with our families for Christmas.

The conclusion of our voyage was uneventful. We put in some long road hours and made better time than we expected. Tim, Eric, and I said our goodbyes where the NY/NJ interstates split, and I drove into the night, bound for Newburgh. I had a few final hours in the dark to reflect and reminisce before the reunion.

When I rang the doorbell, Mom's face lit up like a fireworks display. Any melancholy I felt was washed under a surge of enthusiasm and genuine joy. We had never been apart for that length of time or had to endure that much distance. She immediately saw the changes and the transformation. It was impossible to hide my new outlook. I could tell she was proud of me for taking chances and succeeding. We stayed up all night, sharing stories and getting back to basics. Even with Los Angeles swimming in my skin, home was always home.

There was this unmistakable combination of confidence and anticipation in the room. Like walking down the ramp after riding a roller coaster, I was beaming with a sense of accomplishment. Four months. Three thousand miles. Afflicted with an unpredictable monster inside, I kept the beast at bay.

THE BALANCE

I DON'T KNOW if it was the mercurial nature of my medical circumstances or simply my age, but my life felt like a washer stuck on spin. Here I was, healthy and back in Ithaca, and all I could think about was the city I'd left behind. A world away from blizzards and gray skies, the smog-laden freeways and eternal beaches of the Pacific were calling me. This was more than California dreaming. A piece of who I was, and who I'd become, was missing.

I wasn't blind to the Ithaca canopy that sheltered us from the harsh realities of the working world. But even without that protection, I knew I could have piloted my way through the city's labyrinth. My total immersion at the record label was proof of my ability to assimilate. This quick-draw adaptability was a useful tool in my arsenal, and the nerve-racking prospects of a life outside my comfort zone were no match for my will to achieve. But any hope of that sunny existence was put on pause. I still had three semesters left on my plate.

Eric and I rented a house off campus and shared the pangs of our return to reality. He was always better at making the best of a tough situation. Where he branched out to rekindle connections, I retreated. Nothing seemed the same, but I was probably just as frustrated with the alterations in my happy Ithaca experience as I was with my own displacement. One of our best friends, Jay, transferred to another school, and a few other connections I thought were solid revealed themselves to be anything but loyal. I wanted everything to feel like home, but home wasn't sitting where I left it.

However, it wasn't all dark days and longing. I focused on my studies, engaged in a brief relationship, and made the most of my junior year. Graduation was coming fast, and my gears were cranking. I'd already resolved to return to the music industry in some capacity, so I had to lay the foundation for my future. The game plan was simple. Stay healthy, finish the semester, and get ready for my collegiate curtain call.

The summer before my senior year was a mixed bag. Keish and I found each other again and rekindled something we both thought we had lost. She recognized changes in me, but her unconditional acceptance for each stage of my growth put us right back on familiar sturdy ground. She was evolving as well, throwing herself into the art curriculum at her school, and I was so proud of her focus and passion. She visited me in Newburgh, and I took a road trip to stay at her mom's house in Virginia. It felt like old times, but I think we both had the sense that this was possibly our last dance. We'd been in and out of each other's lives long enough to acknowledge that a shared intuitive energy could always replace words.

Sadly, the prospect of future medical trouble continued to occupy far too much of my focus. Before this romantic reunion, I had a consultation with a doctor at Memorial Sloan Kettering Cancer Center in Manhattan. There was an idea rattling around in my head that desperately needed some closure. I couldn't stop wondering if there were a way to remove whatever was blocking my ventricles, thus eliminating the need for shunting altogether. We had been given various hypotheses about what precipitated my hydrocephalus, but there never seemed to be any definitive diagnosis. So if someone could eliminate the cause, they could eliminate the symptoms. Made sense to me.

But that is why I'm not a neurosurgeon. It was explained that the location of the supposed blockage was in a delicate and fairly restricted surgical zone. Only under the most extreme cases would a scalpel or laser go anywhere near the brain stem. The risks far outweighed the benefits, and the removal of the blockage could cause a formation of scar tissue bigger than the blockage itself. Hence, a shunt would be needed anyway. Ironically, this was one of the very early postulations presented at Westchester before my first procedure. But this time, it seemed more grounded, more definite.

It was disappointing, but it's hard to argue with logic. This heartbreaker was delivered by one of the leading doctors in the field of neuro-oncology, so I trusted that his deductions came from a place of experience. Actually, he questioned whether there was a glioma present at all. If so, he concluded, it must be near microscopic. He even posed that the cause of my hydrocephalus could have been aqueductal stenosis, a narrowing of the aqueduct required for transportation of the CSF from one ventricle to another. It might just be a case of bad anatomy. I thanked him for the information and decided to continue my shunted, somewhat stunted, life.

My regular daily existence was like walking a trail littered with pitfalls. I had to constantly evaluate and navigate. Maybe it was a pipe dream to think anything could change, but each consultation or article about a surgical breakthrough cracked open the door to possibility. Each time that door closed, a piece of that hope retreated.

I've never had an easy time with the concept of living in the moment, embracing the human condition one day at a time, or ignoring tomorrow for today. I dwell and obsess, and that compulsive need to predict outcomes in an unpredictable world stood in direct odds with any notion of a healthy reality. So I routinely shot myself in the foot, doing things the same way and expecting a different result. It was the very definition of insanity.

Some of this was hardwired and some of it was studied, but it was all a part of my functional dysfunction. I wanted to believe there was some great lesson to be learned from this struggle. I needed to be sure that all the pain and fear and worry existed purposely to cover me with some kind of protective coating. I hoped that the rest of life's little obstacles would seem insignificant in the shadow of everything

I'd faced. But I couldn't fully allow myself to surrender my ironfisted logic. There were always the dark whispers from the shadows. You're broken. You're flawed. You're simply not as good as the rest. Stop lying to yourself. Wake up.

This push and pull continued throughout my senior year, but it wasn't strictly medical. There was a consistent battle between the person I was and the person I wanted to be. Often this perception was only slightly incongruent. But the last year of a college education is heavy with decision making and planning, all while attempting to capture mental photographs of these singularly rare experiences. The ticking clock was setting off a panic alarm.

I was in a relationship that started in the winter and steadily evolved into the spring. She was my escape and my safety net. We found ample common ground, and I relished the fact that my plans with her allowed me to run from my roommates and sink into a private world of our own creation. I will always regret some of those lost moments with Eric, and I wish I'd been better at incorporating Nikki into the fold. It was purely my inability to see the big picture, and I was too soaked in my own petty irritations to comprehend how quickly time melts away. College feels eternal until it ends, and then we're left wondering where four years of our lives disappeared.

As Nikki and I grew closer, I realized something substantial was flourishing. It was a new kind of connection, vastly different from the brief, interrupted time I spent with my LA Jenny or the considerable history I had with Keish. I felt so comfortable so quickly. Nikki was cool and spontaneous, and we both had just enough crazy to keep things interesting. We bonded over music, film, and a natural predisposition to see the absurdity in the world. The union grabbed us both by surprise, but we embraced it as a gift and held on to the wheel.

As my Ithaca experience began its final descent, many of my friends and classmates were scrambling for jobs and white-knuckling through interviews. It was crunch time, and there was a noticeable shift in the school's senior class stress level. Eric, like many of the LA program alumni, was headed back to Hollywood. He wasn't letting any grass grow under his feet and planned on flying out shortly after graduation. He had already spent the summer after our internships in LA with Tim. They rented a studio apartment, found an agent, and even got some regular extra work on a major feature film. They'd gotten very comfortable with Los Angeles culture, and I envied their exploits when I visited them on Eric's birthday.

However, my life took a slightly different trajectory. Because of my experience working at the indie record label, I was fortunate enough to secure a position at one of the biggest music companies in the world. It was an incredibly exciting opportunity. Plus, the fact that this job was solidified in January lightened the weight of any second-semester anxiety. For once, it was nice not chasing my own tail and finally feeling ahead of the curve. My creative juices were flowing, and I figured my time at the label could kill two birds with one stone. I would gain experience and knowledge about the inner workings of the industry while building connections to utilize later in the game. So my LA dreams were put on pause as Manhattan came into focus.

Part of that picture included Nikki, and after some lengthy discussions, we decided to close our eyes and leap by moving in together. Well, technically, she moved into the house with Mom and me, but it was still pretty significant. She wanted to experience living closer to the city, and I certainly wasn't ready to end things after graduation. It seemed like a feasible and mutually beneficial solution. I knew I would be commuting from Newburgh to Manhattan each day, returning to Nik and Mom each night, and saving money for whatever came next.

Shortly after graduation, Nik and I took a vacation to Seattle to celebrate the completion of school by visiting the famous music museum, seeing some shows, and unwinding before the move. We shared an unquenchable thirst for music, so it was a trip we both eagerly anticipated. As a rule, nerves and restlessness peak whenever I'm taken out of my environment or routine. But the night I spent at Nikki's house in Niagara Falls before our Seattle flight shot the word *anxiety* into the stratosphere.

I was wide-eyed, my mind spinning with insomnia, tossing and turning on her couch. I wanted to justify the apprehension by convincing myself it was the garden-variety uneasiness I always experienced before I had to fly. It was part worry, part fear. I never liked being too many miles away from my surgeons, and Seattle was about as far as I could get. But I felt pretty good, so there was something more pressing fueling my panic. As dawn arrived, so did some clarity. The finality of our decision to live together was strangling me. I was trapped.

The topic wasn't discussed as we prepared for our week on the West Coast. As two opinionated individuals, we often traded verbal blows and refused to concede defeat. This was a pattern that we repeated too often and one that ultimately proved toxic to the relationship. Seattle was no exception. Laughing one minute and crying the next, our relationship was a lot of fun and a lot of drama. I guess that's what people call passion. I call it foreshadowing.

The break-up/make-up seesaw continued throughout the moving process, and our early Newburgh days were painted with layers of tedious bickering and a strange sibling-like rivalry. I suppose the introduction of someone else into the house forced us into more traditional familial roles. But Mom never signed up to play mediator and disciplinarian to two adults. She raised one child. She had no desire to rewind the clock and try for two.

However, because I was in the city so much of the day, Nik and Mom bonded quickly and became quite close. She was Nik's defender when she felt my feelings or behaviors were unjustified. This certainly upset the power dynamic, and there was a part of me that resented the disruption of our established balance. Still, I understood Mom's sensitive nature and careful logic better than my own. She would protect Nikki, but her loyalty remained faithfully in my camp. Our team was ironclad.

But Nik and I had plenty of good days and shared some rare, wonderful moments together. It took time, but we fostered a genuine connection. We could read each other's thoughts without asking and understood what fed the heart and where the cracks were weakest.

Often, we chose to ignore those truths in place of a juvenile power war. For whatever reason, the mundane battles were the coal that fed the fire to fuel the ship. Similarities in personality and perception are what drove us both crazy.

The resolve of my sometimes-emotional stubbornness was put to the ultimate test during the September 11th tragedy. My surgeries consistently taught me lessons about perspective and valuing the important moments in life. But the raw power of the world literally rattling under my feet was almost ineffable. I didn't hear about hijacked planes on TV or read about fuel fires online. I watched from my seat on the train near Harlem as the first tower hurled smoke into the sky. I watched it collapse into the ground from a big screen in the record label's lobby. This wasn't a disaster across the globe or across the country. This was Manhattan. It was right in my backyard.

The events of that day are documented well enough, and I could write a dissertation about the global significance, but that's not the purpose here. The only world we ever truthfully know is our own. Everything outside of individual consciousness is only perception. So I can only give an account of how I was personally impacted.

Holed up in the offices of the label, we watched the world's most hyperactive city grind to a crawl. The occasional taxi, blowing through the streets like tumbleweed, replaced Broadway's unending procession of buses and pedestrians. Our eyes were glued to television sets and discontinued subway schedules, trying to make sense of the chaos. Cell towers were disabled and the office phone lines worked sporadically. To be in a city of millions of people with millions of questions was incredibly unsettling. New York is famous for its palpable energy, and that day was no exception. We clung to one another for support and tried to traverse a jungle of uncertainty.

Eventually, the trains leaving Manhattan started running again, so I made my way down to Grand Central Station. Still shaken, I decided to avoid any potential danger underground by walking. It was only about a mile away, and I needed some air and some time to process the insanity of what I'd seen.

Less than three blocks from my office, I could already spot the thick plumes of black smoke riding on the wind like some oncoming sandstorm. It was hard to believe how massive and intimidating it looked from that far away. I couldn't imagine staring up at those buildings from street level and watching them crumble. The universe has ways of telling us how small and insignificant we are. This reminder was man-made, and I felt like an ant under a work boot. It's rare to be entirely present in the moment, but I knew this was a picture that would reside in my heart forever.

The bustle and buzz of the regular commuter trains along the Hudson was silenced. We were packed in like cattle, but you could hear a penny drop. By the time I boarded, it was standing room only. So I balanced myself in the aisle, the density of collective thoughts keeping me upright. Heads bowed. Eyes on the floor. Tissues wiping tears. It was the longest seventy-eight minutes of my life.

I had very brief contact with Mom and Nik during the day, finding small windows when the landlines were working. It was just enough communication to know we were all okay. But she was anxious to have her son out of the city and back home where the three of us could hold on to some semblance of safety. Whatever that word meant, we weren't sure.

I counted myself lucky that day and returned to Newburgh with a recalibrated sense of perspective. Normally, I juggled the uncertainties of my own life. This time, the wariness was on a much larger scale. It wasn't about controlling the uncontrollable or coping with the inconveniences of my condition. This was global survival. It marked the first in a series of actions that definitively changed the world. We spent the night grateful for our heartbeats, glued to news streams, and comforted by conversation.

The record label was closed for the rest of the week. We all needed some time to exhale. When I returned the following Monday, the weight and worry of the city hung on me like an oversized parka. The trains were silent. Commuters stared at their shoes, lost in reflection. The eager, sometimes angry populace of New York was reduced to a parade of speechless drones. Nothing felt the same. I was angry, and I was hurt. We wanted answers, and we wanted someone to pay.

For the first few days, we huddled in the VP's office, just talking and, more importantly, listening. Many of the employees in my department were born and raised in the city, and hell hath no fury like a New Yorker scorned. We leaned on one another, trying to extract an explanation from all the broken pieces. The hours evaporated, and we realized that being at work didn't necessarily mean any work would be done. It was far more important that we felt connected when everything around us felt torn apart. Actually, it was incredibly cathartic, and I know that those days will live in me. For as tragic as those times were, the unwavering unity shown by the people of that city was remarkable. I was so proud to be an *almost* New Yorker.

There are many images and thoughts burned into my memories from that time. One night, I pulled onto my street after work and saw Mom and Nik standing on the front steps of our house holding lit candles. It was a sign of support for the affected families. The rest of the neighborhood was dark, but they stood proudly, following the requests of a local effort to show solidarity with the city. There was sadness in the message and the gesture. I joined them immediately.

Our souls felt broken. In New York, sidewalk vigils were everywhere. Posters and pictures of the fallen heroes and missing families were plastered on any available piece of real estate. There was an overwhelming wave of respect and reverence. But a sense of helplessness and frustration over the inability to rewind the clock permeated the city. This black cloud of grief enveloped Manhattan and there wasn't enough light left to see the bright side.

In a weird way, I feel kind of lucky that I was there to experience it. As awful as those early days were, the fact that I was able to live inside a piece of history is rare. It was a study in the human condition and a prime example of how high the unbreakable spirit can soar in times of need. We are so much stronger than we know. If we refuse to be toppled, we'll continue to stand. I took that lesson with me and stored it for future use.

THE LAKE EFFECT

I WAS GOOD at my job. I loved Manhattan. Music was everything to me. Being back home with Mom in Newburgh was a comfortable fit. But something wasn't quite right. Nik and I had some real rocky days, and the highs weren't rescuing the lows anymore. We forced ourselves to make an effort, but the results were minimal. There was an emptiness I just couldn't fill. I thought with enough distraction, I would eventually find a rhythm to quell the voices of longing. Unfortunately, that's not the way it works. Discover a way to appease those voices or they'll just continue to scream.

The artist's spirit is a difficult thing to suppress. Just when you think you have a handle on the balance between work and freedom, the scales tilt. The coins fall. Each hour on that train, in that desk, was another hour of lost opportunity. The master plan of working my way up in the industry, building connections, and ultimately moving into one of New York's many songwriter circles was fast becoming a speck of dust in the distance. I felt the blueprint slipping away. Stuck in restricted parking, I was just an observer with a stopwatch. It was time to feed the meter.

In an attempt to scratch my creative itch, I filled notebooks with poetry, musings, and rudimentary song sketches, I tried to teach myself the keyboard, and I recorded scratch vocal melodies on a handheld recorder whenever inspiration struck. Basically, I put tiny Band-Aids on bigger bruises. It was a way to stave off the hunger. But time management was never my strong suit, so the weeks continued to click away. I needed life to shake me up, nonmedically, for once.

The more Nik and I recognized that our relationship was sinking with quicksand speed, the less sense it made for her to stay with me in Newburgh. The ultimate decision that she would move back to Buffalo came fairly quickly. It wasn't like we had a bounty of options. We both wanted a change in our situation and a break from each other.

I'm sure the life she imagined was filled with weekends in the city, endless discussions about art, film, and music, and the general feeling that she had a partner in the trenches. Although there were a number of factors responsible, this is certainly not what she got. Effort is everything, and it was too easy to put the operating system to sleep. Falling into a pattern of apathy and distraction will derail even the best-laid plans.

But Nik and I lived on a pendulum, trading exasperation for love in the blink of an eye. Sometimes the swings were unthinkable, but that was how we functioned. After some final fights and plenty of tears, Nik made her way back to Western NY. I had one foot out the door of the label, but no next step. Then the pendulum swung.

Long discussions on the phone prompted radical action, and Nikki proposed that I give Buffalo a test drive. There was a smaller more manageable music scene, and the cost of living was a fraction of what I would pay in NY. It was a big leap, and everyone at work thought I was crazy. But they respected an artist pursuing his art. I wanted a life of options and open doors. I wanted the best with Nik. So we found the edge for the second time and jumped.

She was a stranger in a strange land when she came to Newburgh. Now, the roles were reversed. I was diving into a pool of the unknown to chase the idea of transformation. Most of that strategy felt insane, but it's easy to be persuaded when you're already reaching for straws. We craved a clean slate, and we hoped a change in scenery could be the catalyst for a relationship revival. I wanted to make music and tap the creative potential living inside. She looked to grow into the kind of woman she conjured in her mind. It was a lot to ask of a town. Maybe too much.

Once again, I left the safety of home for new real estate. As with my trip to Los Angeles, a defiance to beat my condition overtook my common sense. It was a conscious choice. I simply refused to be hampered by my head. I settled into the Snowbelt with an energetic anticipation for all Buffalo had to offer. Life was nothing but blank pages and unanswered questions, and I couldn't have wanted that more. My doubts swam upstream as fear fueled every stroke. It was an experience I needed, embraced, and then vacillated about constantly.

The yin and the yang. The blinding light and the chilling black. This was where I learned to lift myself up, simply to destroy a flawed foundation. For the first time, I felt the sting of the introspective artist. The thrill of potential straining to hold the free fall of defeat. Too much time to think. Too much time to question. I was constructing a comfort zone of solitude, staying safe in my established routine. But life is an uncontrollable, unpredictable thing. The more tightly I held on to my compulsions, the more entrenched I became. It was a false sense of freedom and an irrational justification for loneliness. But I followed my own playbook and assumed things would magically fall into place. Some dangerous patterns emerged during those long gray winters.

Nikki and I tried to inject some new life into the relationship, but the strain of our shifted power dynamic (and my own eagerness for a fresh creative start) put too great a tax on our living situation. It was shocking how thoroughly our roles were reversed. She was in her environment, in her apartment, with a steady job and the proximity of family. I was looking for work, scraping by, and was now more than six hours from home. She understood the motivation at the root of my situation and she was extremely supportive, but everyone's shoulders eventually get sore from carrying the burden of expectation. The old issues were still there, with a new environment to contaminate. It always came down to effort and attention, but we were too young, too stubborn, and too shortsighted to let down our defenses and acquiesce.

I had a job selling season ticket packages for the Buffalo Philharmonic Orchestra, but the part-time pay was minimal. I was lucky to pull together enough to contribute to rent. It was a radical lifestyle shift, but I did my best to convince myself it was part of the dues-paying process. I expected to look back at those days and appreciate the struggle. It was never easy to justify the means when I was stuck in the middle of the grind, but I tried to maintain focus and spin my wheels out of the mud. This was a long and tedious undertaking.

After a few fizzled projects with more talk than action, I settled into my role as lead vocalist and lyricist for an all-original band. It was nearly impossible to find musicians who focused on original songs in place of covers, but a guitarist named Ed saw one of my flyers in a local music store and decided to take a chance. Ed was an older established guitar player, but his passion for growth and his instrumental skills were impressive. His son was also a gifted player, and I think Ed hoped to bring him into the fold. Ultimately, that never happened, but Ed and I forged a bond over mutual respect and an admiration for each other's talents. We spent endless hours in his upstairs rehearsal studio, crafting melodies and building the foundation for our sound. The plan was to create the songs, recruit additional members to flesh out the arrangements, and bring a strong, authentic sound to an area seriously lacking original music.

In a town of strangers, Ed, his wife Diane, and their family became a surrogate safety blanket. I will always be grateful for their open arms and willingness to accept me into the fold. I tried to repay them by bringing a new energy and fresh outlook to their lives. They were born and raised in a linear town that was saddled with a homogeneous perspective, so I offered a glimpse of a few hills and valleys. I desperately needed the stability of a home base, so we complemented each other well. I felt a part of something special. But the reality of my situation was another matter.

Nikki's sister got her a waitressing job at a sports bar to help supplement her income. Our relationship was wobbling on its last leg, but it was financially necessary for us to stay together. That predicament changed when I started working at the same bar. I could now afford to get my own place and lessen the tension germinated from forced cohabitation. We could still hang at work without the strain of constantly being in each other's space. At that time, it seemed like an ideal situation. But it was just temporary glue to hold the broken pieces together.

Living on my own for the first time was fantastic. I'm not the kind of person who thrives in crowded, hectic living environments. Some people love that energy and the constant contact. I am an only child with a plethora of carefully constructed systems, structures, and habits. There is a tangible sense of peace I can achieve by living in my own head, in my own space. I had a single room in Ithaca, but it was in a typical college dorm. I lived with roommates during my internship in LA, housemates for my last two years in school, and then with Nik and Mom in Newburgh. Living with Nikki in Buffalo completed a long history of shared occupancy. Now, I was free to fly, and it was liberating.

There was always a concern about being too isolated with my medical condition. A certain safety net existed when there were others around me aware of my situation. When things got bad, the decline happened quickly. My sophomore year scare was a good example. I was alone and teetering on the edge. If it wasn't for outside intervention, I would have drifted into a deep unconscious sleep. Even in that debilitated state, I knew I was slipping away. The effects could have been devastating. Luck and timing are very important things.

The brain is the mainframe. It controls all analysis, decision making, and movement. Crack the motherboard and the system will crash. Pull the plug, and it's straight to shutdown. But assuming the computer can somehow repair itself alone is absurd. I had an infrastructure that routinely tiptoed along the edge of malfunction. Thinking my condition would disappear because it was more convenient for my solitary lifestyle was ignorant, shortsighted, and irresponsible. It was crazy. So by packing up my things and waving goodbye to the safety of Nik's apartment, I guess I was deciding to get a little nuts.

I can't say there were any major scares while I lived with Nikki, but there were definitely a few reminders. Without as much money, the gym membership was gone. So I no longer had the crutch of lifting weights to flush out the intracranial pressure. Sometimes I got headaches. Bad headaches. I never had migraines, but from what I've heard, they bear a resemblance. Nearly paralyzing, my head would pound, my eyes would blur, and a wave of exhaustion forced me into recovery sleep. That was my only respite. I had to shut out the world to sleep away the pain.

But reminders never registered as warnings. I was far too busy convincing myself I was healthy to see any signs contrary to my created truth. I believed I could think away my physical impediments, and this was long before I legitimately explored using the mind for healing. Ignoring symptoms and hoping they'd stop was the plan. It was wishful thinking, not focused energy.

Life continued without interruption for a while. The band gained momentum despite a rotating roster of members. Ed and I did our best to make our mark on the local scene. Diane was a fantastic sounding board, and we became genuine kindred spirits. My nightly shifts at the sports bar kept me running, delivering some significant friendships and a wholly unique new relationship with a fellow server named Christine. I settled into a rhythm I didn't necessarily think I would have found. So I ignored the periphery and tried to find some distant finish line. There were flashes of hope and moments of happiness, but the chasm between dreams and reality was unambiguous. This was not supposed to be my life.

At a certain point, I decided to look for a Buffalo-based neurosurgeon. I knew I had been toying with fate, and it just didn't make sense to leave a last-minute decision for the emergency room. I wanted the power to carefully choose my own brain carpenter. I'd been in enough offices and had seen enough hospitals to roughly gauge a doctor's competence and compatibility from an initial impression. Plus, because I was walking around with a very specific kind of programmable valve, I couldn't pick just any surgeon off the street. My doctor needed to be warm, understanding, compassionate, skilled, and an impeccable medical genius. Small order. I set out to find a Western NY miracle worker.

The first meeting didn't leave me with high hopes. This particular physician told me that he didn't "necessarily prefer" my type of valve and that there was no medical evidence proving it was any more successful than standard valves. Basically, the system that had saved my life for the last three-and-a-half years was nothing more than a generic piece of plastic without real merit. I was dismissed. "Run along son. No one in this area would use a valve like that." Translation: "I'm not qualified to install this particular unit, so I'm going to downplay its effectiveness." I left angry and dejected.

But just a few days later, I found my saving grace. Sometimes a little research goes a long way. Apparently, only two surgeons in the Buffalo area were certified to install the programmable valve, so I made an appointment with the first doctor accepting new patients.

This experience was the total antithesis of what I endured three days before. Dr. S praised the reliable usefulness and utility of my valve. He recounted a number of his cases where the buildup of debris caused a genuine concern, and this valve eradicated that issue. He spoke to me like a friend and promised that if anything should happen, he would be there to make the necessary corrections. It was exactly what I needed to hear. So I walked out into some rare Buffalo sunshine and felt the warm reassurance of my newly installed safety net.

With any immediate health concerns pacified, I turned my focus back to life as a struggling artist. Then, one night I had an epiphany. Maybe part of this isolation, depression, and general mode of dissatisfaction had less to do with my station and more to do with basic hardwiring. Would I be happier somewhere else? Was my lack of forward momentum a result of my surroundings or was it the cause? In a perfect world, with perfect health, does the game change? Was

I wasting valuable creative years in an area I never even planned on calling home? I had some serious soul-searching on the agenda.

I started to knock around the idea of moving to New York. My days in Buffalo made me thirsty for a bigger and more heterogeneous city. I was sick of treading water. I missed the energy of Manhattan, and I wanted to swim in a forward-thinking, progressive arts community. I'd been able to leapfrog the roadblocks that Buffalo placed in my path, and it felt like time for a change. So I put together a game plan to shed my Erie County skin and head for greener pastures. But every adventure comes at a cost.

It wasn't just a matter of packing some bags and making the drive. I had an established life there, albeit one I needed to leave behind. An exit from Buffalo meant ending my current relationship, dissolving the band, saying goodbye to Nikki, and leaving Brian, one of the closest and truest friends I'd ever had.

With no definitive deadline, I knew I could take the days needed to get these affairs in order. I didn't want to spend any more transition time than necessary, but scheduling the move was entirely up to me. Once my mind was set on anything, I went into cruise control. My days were numbered, but I wanted to leave as painlessly as possible.

The first step was breaking the news to Ed. This was difficult for me because meeting Ed and forming that band gave me some incredibly valuable and memorable experiences. Plus, this decision affected not only me, but theoretically changed the lives of three other members of the group. I had been exploring areas of personal discontent through my lyrics long before I made any final resolution to leave, but I'm sure the other guys just chalked those up to poetic expression. They most likely figured it was the practice of venting frustration through writing. Unfortunately, the pages in those notebooks were packed with more authentic desperation than compositional fantasy.

I was nervous to broach the subject with Ed, so I took the slightly cowardly alternative and confided in Diane. We had grown very close, and we were well aware of Ed's passion (and passive-aggressive nature). I didn't want him to lock up, shut off, and resent me. So

I thought if Diane cushioned the blow by giving him an abridged version of the story, I could fill in the details later. This was probably not the best idea, but I was young and I felt bad about abandoning a project we both worked so hard to create. In hindsight, it was simply another life lesson I needed to learn before I left.

Ed normally picked me up in his van, and we made the trip across the lake to our drummer's house for practices. In the beginning, we spoke like daydreamers, fantasizing about playing on The Tonight Show or picturing what it would be like to tour the country. The glue that held this band together was the fact that Ed and I attacked everything we did with an unwavering focus and professionalism rarely seen in music or life in general. For whatever reason, I possessed the foresight to recognize opportunities and the energy and passion to see those plans to fruition. Ed shared that vision, but his diligence grew from a life of experience and perfectionism.

Over time, these mini-voyages took a noticeably quieter turn. Conversations centered more on upcoming local gigs, stories about work, or random current events. It was filler. Real life took the place of fantasy. The dream of making music started to feel a little too much like business.

A good band is a small group of strong relationships. There's intimacy and trust. There's romance. It's a marriage. When the spark starts to fade, you can feel it. Even if no one addresses the obvious, it's palpably painful. The elephant in the room takes a seat on your face. Ed and I were both quietly aware of the shift. The tension grew each practice night. But after the talk with Diane, those drives began to physically hurt.

I have a good heart, so maybe a part of me just felt bad for dropping the news so suddenly. But I also knew when I reached my saturation point, and there was no way I could have fooled myself into believing this project, or my existence in Buffalo, had any real chance of growth. It was time to lay down my hand and walk away from the table.

After a number of semi-awkward practices and increasingly muted van rides, Ed finally broke the silence on the way home one night. He told me about the discussion he had with Diane and how surprised he was that I'd decided to leave. He assumed I was going to stay with my girlfriend, continue playing with the band, and build a life for myself. Because we were so often on the same page, I was shocked he never recognized the warning signs or sensed my frustration. Maybe he was just blinded by the light of wishful thinking. Maybe I hid it better than I thought.

After the news was out in the open, the situation relaxed considerably. It became a secret that Ed and I shared, and we both decided there was no point in telling the other guys this early in the game. We still had scheduled shows, and we wanted those last months to be productive and fun without any looming dark clouds. Ed and I got to work and put renewed energy into the goal of finishing strong.

With the news of my exit, my relationship with Christine dissolved. It was difficult to stay invested when an expiration date was on the table. I did my best to keep things amicable, but we had been through a lot together, and it was pretty impossible for both of us to feel wildly happy about the decision to hit the brakes. In our mutual attempt to be mature, we remained in casual contact until the end, but that early magic was gone. Relationships are often most remembered for their beginnings. Those beginnings with her were some of the best.

My friend Brian and I had become incredibly close, and even though there were a lot of people and experiences I was going to miss, nothing was more important than my friendship with him. What started as a simple connection through work blossomed into the kind of bond I never believed I'd find in the heavy homogeny of Buffalo, NY. We were both thinkers and dreamers, with our eyes set deep in the distance. We loved the same music and looked at the world through similar lenses. Brian played the role of confidant and sounding board, and I returned the favor. Sometimes we were buried in introspection, sometimes lost in absurdity. We complemented and supported each other during a period when we both had a lot of questions about the future. It was a brief snapshot of two unlikely souls finding each other in the most unlikely of places. Brian ultimately decided to stay in the area and raise a family. I miss the uniqueness of what we had, and I still think about him all the time.

A couple of months before I left, I took a trip to LA. My core crew from Ithaca as well as a significant "friends of friends network" was all there at that point, and I was thirsty for a reconnection. Phone contact was minimal with our fluctuating work patterns, contrasting schedules, and different time zones, so I wanted to remember what it felt like to be back with my base. It didn't take long.

This visit was a hurricane of memories and emotions. I knew I missed these guys. I just didn't know I missed them this much. There's no truer test of a friendship than distance and time. Walking off that plane and into this new world they created was overwhelming. Having spent so many days living at a slower speed, it was easy to forget the pace and energy of a major city. Everything I cherished about my experiences in California returned, with a more adult makeover. I already loved LA. Now, I loved *their* LA.

It was a virtual Ithaca reunion, and I was so grateful that the transplants made an effort to get together. I bathed in a warm pool of support, and I was happy to see that the group had added some new members. Eric's friend Matt (who I'd first bonded with during those trips down to the Jersey Shore after our freshman year) moved to LA with his roommate Stuart. Stuart had become as close a member of this family as anyone, and I absolutely understood why he was brought into the fold. From our first meeting, I had a feeling this was someone who would play a significant part in my life. Intuition is a powerful thing.

I hung with people I hadn't seen since graduation. I was so proud of everyone for diving into the unknown to follow artistic dreams. My little band in my little city felt even smaller and less significant. It certainly didn't take that trip for me to realize I wasn't living the life I intended, but it definitely put that fact into focus. Maybe being the tortoise in the race would turn out for the best. Maybe I needed to learn valuable lessons about perseverance and struggle. Maybe delaying the gratification of California's sunshine by suffocating in some Buffalo blizzards helped me understand the importance of patience. Regardless of the results, one thing was now certain. I wasn't moving to New York. I was heading to LA.

It just made sense. Starting from scratch in a city like New York would have put me right back into the rut of loneliness and isolation born from apartment living. I craved my support core, and that core wasn't close. There are stories about people who get off a Greyhound with a suitcase and a dream, but I knew I required more than aspiration. I like a little concrete in the foundation of my decisions.

I needed to lean on someone and let them lean back. Eric, the constant rock, recognized that longing. Through tears, I said goodbye, with promises of a permanent return within the year. It was time to finalize the exit from Buffalo, establish a base camp back in Newburgh, and tell Mom I was moving 3,000 miles away.

THE BOILING POINT

THE BLUEPRINT WAS simple but loaded. Move back to Newburgh, find a restaurant gig, save some money, align my ducks, and head out west. Completely change my life and my environment. Roll the dice. Hope for the best. But the universe consistently found a way to modify a misguided course. It only hurt when I tried to push against the grain.

I had a fairly clear idea of my time frame. I calculated the amount of money I would need to get a car and still maintain enough of a cushion for the first few months without steady work. There were a number of loose ends and unanswered questions, but that made the move even more exhilarating. It also helped that I was at the frayed end of my Buffalo rope and was more than ready for a change.

Mom still believed my final destination was New York. Telling her that I was leaving was going to be the stickiest part of my plan. This wasn't a three-hour trip to Ithaca or a six-hour ride to Buffalo. This was the other side of the country, and for us, it could have been the other side of the world. It wasn't for a semester or a week in the summer. This was for keeps.

I knew I needed to handle the news with care. She understood my desire to leave Western New York, and she supported my passion for pursuing a life in the arts. The city was only an hour away, and

I'd already established a certain level of familiarity with the boroughs from my days at the record label. But it was no place for the weak-willed, and you ate what you killed in Manhattan. Living in New York was romantic, but living in LA was doable. I didn't have the luxury of prolonged decision making or money to burn. It was time to come clean.

Shortly after I got settled at home, I asked Mom if we could go to a small intimate bistro in town to talk. She knew me too well not to be suspicious. This was a serious discussion, and there was a definite weight to my words. I was pretty nervous, but the resolve behind my decision helped me get the message across. I wasn't sitting on the fence. My heart was already in LA.

It certainly wasn't easy. We both shed some tears and tried to let the gravity of the situation register. She said she knew how much I loved California and she understood my need to be back with my core support team. There was emptiness and a void inside that desperately needed to be filled. She didn't want me to suffer anymore, and if that meant letting me fly, she was willing to bear the pain. It was a shock and a slap in the soul, but she heard my voice change when I got back from my last trip. She saw a renewed spirit and enthusiasm normally nonexistent in my isolated tundra. She didn't want to lose me. But if I stayed, I would continue to be lost.

The job hunt was relatively smooth. I had a couple of leads but solidified a position as a server in a newly opened Greek restaurant. It was family-owned and operated, the polar opposite of my corporate sports bar experience. I wanted to focus on more personal interactions as a waiter in a warm inviting environment. I liked the idea of being on the ground floor of a business with potential, offering my input and building a mutually beneficial schedule. It was an ideal situation for saving money while working close to home.

The transition was a little rattling. Although I knew my move was temporary, feeling a certain level of regression was unavoidable. I could rationalize and justify my motives, but it still seemed like taking a step back into the protective shell. The safety was, indeed, a blanket.

I wrapped myself in a warm cocoon of familiarity. Living at home is very comfortable, and that's precisely the problem.

Almost instantly, my head went back to Keish. It was impossible for me to walk those halls and sleep in that room and not summon the memories of everything we shared. It happened every time, like a visit from some Ghost of Relationships Past. I knew that she was living in the area, but I didn't know where to find her. We had some brief conversations while I was in Buffalo, and it felt like there was honest potential for a rekindling. But after I canceled plans to see her because of my involvement with Christine, the camel's back finally broke.

With my tail between my legs, I made a delicate first move by sending her a laconic e-mail. I didn't even know if she still used that address, but it was the only line I could throw. I kept the message brief, and that's saying a lot coming from the king of venting through writing. It was an update and a notice that I was back in town. I assumed the message would be met with a certain degree of resistance, but I couldn't stifle what was inevitably going to surface. I did my best to be clear and apologetic and crossed my fingers for a response.

I received a quick reply explaining that she wasn't exactly sure how I would fit into her life again, but she would take some time to think and call me soon. It was surprising and promising, and I was infused with a nostalgic eagerness to see her. Timing is everything, and I felt this could be a viable second chance. Then, the phone rang on Christmas morning.

All of the butterflies assembled in my stomach took flight. I couldn't believe my ears, and most of what I heard sounded fairly optimistic. It wasn't a wide open door, but Keish had cracked it just enough to let in some light. There was still a piece of her that needed to know if the memories she clung to through the countless storms were still alive. I guess I needed to know too.

I stopped by her work on New Year's Day. She appeared from around a corner and I froze. Looking into her eyes after so much time apart was almost too powerful to process. This was Keish. My

Keish. Finally. I wanted to hold her and apologize and wipe the slate clean. I wanted to explain and justify and excuse all of my juvenile decisions and shortsightedness. I wanted to make her feel like we were seventeen again, walking through a world of possibilities. Instead, I mumbled a few lame jokes and battled the awkwardness with a smile. But through the fog of silence and self-consciousness, we made plans to get together later that night. A much-needed reconciliation was only hours away and my heart was pounding.

It was a short drive over the Hudson River to Beacon. Keish was living with roommates, but no one was home. There was a lot on our respective plates, and it took some time to warm up the engines of conversation. The first order of business was recognizing, and ultimately removing, any tension in the room. It was sucking up the oxygen and getting hard to breathe.

It was a bit of a tennis match, but when we actually served each other some honesty, the discussion found familiar ground. She wanted answers, and I wanted the opportunity to explain. It wasn't easy. I had a list of misguided actions to defend and more to justify, sometimes even to myself. But with each piece of disclosure, we moved a little nearer to what we knew was still whispering inside. There was a communion that grew from history. We were hardwired to remember.

She wasn't blameless, but most of the fumbles came from my hands. We had been a part of each other's lives, in one form or another, for a long time. We always had chemistry, but rarely managed to align the intensity of our feelings. Immaturity, distractions, and the general business of life all played a part. But I felt grounded and cleansed, and I was ready to stack the bricks again. Our roots were strong. We just needed some repairs. Keish, on the other hand, had a slightly different idea of how to use those bricks. She chose to build a wall.

The rude awakening that accompanied the arrival of harsh daylight after hours of candles and shadows couldn't compete with the blatant uneasiness we both felt in the room. We spent the night on a constant swing. Silence broke the chatter. Laughter replaced the sad. We started as a spark and grew to a blaze. Secrets shared, secrets kept. We lost and found ourselves in sixteen hours.

The mood in the morning was definitely different. I spoke to her roommate, who I had known since high school, but there was a lingering discomfort I couldn't quite pinpoint. I felt like Keish was rushing to get away from something. I had to hold on to the hope that that something wasn't me. Through a few forced jokes at her door, I grinned and slinked away. I couldn't predict the future, and I had no idea what was waiting for me. But I never assumed that exit would be the first in a series of last goodbyes.

I got back to the house and thought about how unpredictable life can be. The more I obsessed about control, the less real influence I seemed to wield over the trajectory of my course. There is only so much any of us can do to construct the bubble, and the most important thing life can teach us is how easily that bubble can pop.

Dismissing the awkwardness of the morning was easy. It wasn't a comfortable setting, and the addition of her roommate only heightened those levels. We just needed to get to know each other again. Yeah. That was the idea. Start slowly. Baby steps and kid gloves. Even though we had just spent the night together, it was time for reintroductions. Our new selves were strangers to the old. This was going to take some effort, but I was willing to put in the work.

Unfortunately, it takes two to tango. Having more than one person on the same page in a relationship is kind of an important detail. Who knew? As much joy as I got from endless daydream romanticizing, the cold dark reality of the situation was impossible to ignore. After a few follow-up phone calls went unreturned, it finally registered that Keish was not interested in exploring any areas of the pond beyond that initial piece of broken ice. She eventually called to more clearly paint that picture with words. It was also precisely the moment my faith in the concept of love began to wither.

Maybe it was because I was finally on the receiving end of the rejection, but this hit me hard. I guess I had always been in the power position, and I took that power for granted. I deserved some retribution, but I would have preferred yelling and screaming to severed ties. The whole conversation happened in slow motion. I just kept waiting for her to concede, but my arguments and pleas fell on deaf ears. She wouldn't cave. She wouldn't retreat. This was sincere. I was losing the love of my life.

It wasn't my finest hour. I hung up the phone, jumped in the car, drove through the pouring rain, and appeared unannounced at her doorstep. A grand gesture of some romantic promise of commitment, I guess. She was confused and a little uncomfortable. From her perspective, we had our discussion, she said what she needed to say, and it was over. Why was I soaking wet standing at the foot of the stairs like an abandoned puppy looking for the leash?

We talked for a little while in her room, but any effort to explain fell flat. I knew it was pointless to convince the inconvincible. I'd used up far too many free passes in our years together. It was time for my sentencing. I dragged my shackles back to the car and sat in the rain. If I pulled out of that driveway, I knew I would never return. This could be the last time I'd see her. My stomach felt hollow, and I was physically drained from the emotional exertion of the night. Eventually, the self-conscious realization that my car was running and my lights were shining on the wall of her apartment was enough to push me back into the street.

The recovery period wasn't immediate, but I eventually cleared some of the emotional residue and tried to refocus on the task at hand. I turned the spare room into a writing/recording space so I could have my own area to be creative. This became a private zone where I could escape, unclutter my head, and expel any residual hurt through healthier outlets than obsession and self-pity. It worked. Sometimes.

A fairly persistent theme of this narrative has been the shock of those unpredictable bolts of lightning that took the legs of a situation already walking through the mud and crippled them. The stamina needed to routinely sweep up the broken pieces should stand as a testament to my strength and resilience. But I've learned that when lightning strikes, something just gets burned.

I continued my work at the restaurant, saving almost everything I made. Living at home was a fast track for accumulating funds. Add the lack of any social distractions and I had a tasty recipe for fiscal responsibility. My core was all in LA, and I maintained very few ties with any hometown high school friends. I had some intensely close relationships throughout my developing years in Newburgh, but when I left for Ithaca (and then Buffalo), those ties weakened. I've never been the best at sustaining connections, especially when distance intervened.

There are a few select friendships I regret dissolving, and those regrets are something I've carried. But a new environment with new scenery sometimes painted the past with a blurry brush. Every step was an original lesson in anticipating what was ahead and remembering what I'd left behind. It was the only way to move forward.

I attempted to keep my blinders attached and my eyes fixed on the finish line. Unfortunately, a methodical planner is the first one to watch his carefully laid plans crumble under the weight of expectation. Waiting tables was simple. Writing music was inspiring. Planning a West Coast rebirth was rejuvenating. Staying after work to flirt with the pretty bartender felt natural and liberating. Doing all of these things while my brain spun like a vertiginous pinwheel proved to be slightly more difficult.

I engineered an old excuse train down familiar tracks. I was probably tired. I hadn't eaten enough. The lights were too harsh. The stress from serving customers was finally getting to me. I'd been exercising a lot lately. The barometric pressure that time of year was a little funky. My allergies were always an issue. But if history had shown me anything, lingering suspicion can't be rationalized away. Positive thinking can't shield the strike when you're slapped with the truth.

When I first moved back to Newburgh from Buffalo, I made an appointment with a neurosurgeon closer to home. I simply wanted to establish a relationship with someone certified in maintaining and installing my programmable valve. Ironically, the doctor I saw was part of my initial neurosurgical team at Westchester. Dr. T hadn't operated on me, but he was one of the first faces I saw in the ER during my "sweatpants consultation." I hadn't even remembered he was the same man until I read through my old medical records.

Because I was without symptoms, it was more of a meet and greet than an actual office visit. But my peace of mind seemed to grow exponentially when a medical contact was one phone call and a few miles away. I was feeling good, so there was no real need to take action or raise any flags. He ordered a CT scan to get a more updated picture of my CSF levels, shunt placement, etc. He reported to my doctor in Buffalo that I seemed to be functioning well, but I didn't have the scans taken until a few weeks later. With hydrocephalus, a world of security can crumble in a few weeks.

Mild headaches and stress-induced strain were usual visitors, but these bouts with dizziness seemed to be something more significant. I couldn't ignore the fact that I wasn't myself. It was like a faint beer buzz or the lightheaded rush from holding my breath for too long. That was my everyday indication that the clouds were gathering. It was tolerable, but uncomfortable and confusing. I needed answers, but didn't want them. I could feel the downward spiral inside me descending like a staircase to oblivion, and there was too much familiarity with that kind of fall.

After the doctor read the results from my CT scan, a phone call for a return office visit came as no surprise. There were daily fluctuations in intensity, but it was absolutely apparent that I had something very wrong with the waterworks. To say that I was eager to see a neurosurgeon about anything is probably inaccurate, but I couldn't keep pretending the storm would pass. At least I could get a game plan organized and begin my search for an ounce of optimism.

Common sense wins again. The heightened fluid levels did, in fact, signal a probable malfunction. Although Dr. T's news was somewhat expected, I couldn't fully process what I was hearing. Confusion. Denial. Anger. Despair. The path lying before me was crawling with landmines. Still, no alternate routes were available. I was about to knowingly walk into the eye of the storm. How did I get back here? How long would I be unfastened from my life? Why must the noose around my neck constrict every time I find some wiggle room to breathe? My neatly woven plans were about to unpleasantly unravel.

However, the fact that this diagnosis was based solely on a perusal of my CT scans provided the thread of hope I needed that a physical exam might offer some workable solutions. A long shot was still a shot. The cards were stacked, and the symptoms were persistent.

But the evolution of technology in the medical field is rapid. A deluge of questions flooded my head. Could some advanced drainage technique buy me more time with this current valve? Have shunt revisions become simpler or have the recovery periods gotten less punishing? I couldn't close the pipe dream door completely, but the outlook was bleak.

Speed was always a factor, and this episode was no exception. Dr. T suggested I travel to Columbia Presbyterian because they had a more extensive neurological facility. Insurance was a major issue, so my options were limited. A possible workaround was to find a surgeon at Westchester Medical where both the doctor and the facility accepted my coverage. Luckily, he had a colleague he believed might be a good fit. After Dr. T arranged a meeting, we raced to find some answers.

I don't remember his name. I probably erased it from my memory. It was an encounter I hoped to instantly forget. Obviously suffering, I walked into his field of vision and he stared at us like we had just interrupted his snack time. Apparently, speaking to someone in need was too heavy a burden for him to bear that day. He abruptly ordered an X-ray to look at the shunt placement, and my intuition said to run. I didn't feel comfortable with him, and I didn't trust his judgment or willingness to help. Then we learned that neither the hospital nor this doctor took my insurance. Instinct wins again. The pot boiled over.

That was enough frustration to spin the sanity ship into orbit. I turned on my heels and headed to the car. I may have needed help, but not *his* kind of help. My tolerance for incompetence was thoroughly exhausted, and I still had no answers, no plan, and no way to numb the pain. It was easy to run away, but it was hard to know when to stop.

I went there with the smallest thread of hope that my valve could be adjusted or, at the very least, I would be given some options. Instead, I was left more alone and lost than ever. I'd felt those little fuses blow before, and this was another example of a malfunctioning brain with far too much on its plate to process. I didn't want to talk. I wouldn't go back inside. I just needed to leave. Mom started the car, and we drove to nowhere.

It wasn't only this incident, but a general realization that my condition was a cycle of hope, loss, regret, anger, damage, and repair. This was another straw in a familiar hay bale of paused dreams and stunted aspirations. I stared out of the window, contemplating, spinning, and lost in disbelief. My options seemed more than limited, practically nonexistent. I could not continue to be a passenger on this ungovernable seesaw. I was cornered. My eyes lost focus. Trees floated by the edge of the parkway. The car felt smaller. Sunlight blinded me from every angle. Oxygen vanished. The anxiety/panic fusion started to surface. Then, the phone rang.

Dr. T heard what happened at Westchester and called with the reassuring mix of concern and levelheadedness that I desperately needed. I wasn't scolded for leaving. He didn't put the sole onus on me to take care of my personal health. He refused to simply wash his hands of the situation, shrug his shoulders, and wish me luck. Instead, he was sympathetic and audibly irritated with the way the encounter was handled. He felt his colleague dropped the ball by not delicately addressing the issues of someone in such a fragile state. I couldn't have agreed more.

To help reconcile things, he scheduled an introduction with the man who would eventually save my life. We had no idea that day that suggesting a consultation with his partner, Dr. K, would set specific wheels in motion that would not only allow me to alleviate the burdens of actual physical pain but would ultimately give me the confidence to leap from that perch of apprehension and finally fly.

We traveled to Northern Westchester Hospital with renewed hope and brighter prospects. Finding someone who was willing to work with me to shape some type of attack plan could help me stop feeling like a pinball bouncing from one opinion to the next. I needed a tactician with skill and a cheerleader with some heart. That combination was difficult to find in a world of left-brainers. But there was one rare dancer who moved to a slightly different beat.

Dr. K didn't look like a neurosurgeon. He had thick hair, modern glasses, and an easy confidence that read more capable than cocky. He had the appearance of a painter, a liberal activist, or some type of bohemian sculptor. The sincerity of his smile and the generosity in his eyes helped warm his face, and I immediately took a step back from the ledge. There was this sensation of instant comfort. I'm not sure why I felt I could trust him so completely. I just knew. My initial reactions are generally proven correct, and this was another example of intuition pushing me down the right path.

He ordered a shunt X-ray to determine whether the tubing was coiled or twisted and a CT scan to inspect my CSF levels. Even though the CT machine was inoperable that day, he examined my valve and determined it might not even be a malfunction. The levels weren't dangerously high, and the valve seemed to depress and refill with fluid. I was sent home and told to return the following day when the CT machine was working.

He also reset my programmable valve to a lower setting to see if the body required a slightly different pressure environment. This was usually a tedious process. The powerful magnet used to adjust the levels from outside the skull was imprecise and often yielded unpredictable results. This was no exception. After three attempts, the new setting was achieved. Fortunately, it was a painless exercise. The only drawback was the disproportionate amount of trips to the X-ray machine to verify that the valve's settings were modified. But a little radiation never killed anyone, right?

We returned the next morning to get the CT scan. That pretty bartender, Jess (who'd now become much more than a work flirt), joined us to hear what I hoped would be some encouraging news. I felt a little better than the day before, so I clung to the possibility that the slight adjustment was some perfectly hidden fix to stop my slide. The effect from pressure fluctuations could be deceiving.

Sometimes the smallest change could drastically tilt the scales, for better or worse.

These scans showed very little variation from the films taken a month earlier. On one hand, this was a good thing because the levels had not significantly increased. However, my hopes of an immediate solution were quickly squashed when it became apparent the valve adjustment was ineffective as well. Dr. K was still hopeful that the debris or excess protein obstructing my flow would eventually pass. He asked that we wait a couple more days, but I was told to call his office if I experienced any exceptional changes. Back home. More waiting. More worries.

Unfortunately, the sleeping giant in this scenario continued to be the insurance situation. The rapidly disappearing sand in my hourglass compounded the stress factor and added some additional weight to an already head-heavy time. As soon as I made the decision to stay with Dr. K, I knew I had to secure insurance from a participating provider. Because it was so dangerous to have a lapse in coverage with a preexisting condition, the transition from one company to another was a tightrope walk. At times, it felt like obstacles were deliberately put in place to sabotage the switch and limit my ability to follow established guidelines. It's not my intention to use this book as a soapbox, but I experienced a health insurance system mired in procedural red tape and confusing medical jargon. For those of us struggling with illness, the additional emotional toll of having to plow through endless fine print was not the medicine we ordered.

The pain and dizziness continued to escalate, so I finally called Dr. K's office two days later. There was an error on the part of his assistant, and he never received the message, but Jess followed up with him later that evening. He was concerned that the pressure had not equilibrated and asked that I report back to Northern Westchester the following morning for another valve adjustment. If at first you don't succeed…

The valve was dialed down, but it wouldn't refill with fluid. It was sluggish to empty a few days earlier, but now seemed completely uncooperative. Dr. K tried to tap it with a syringe, but no CSF escaped. This meant there was definitely a blockage. A procedure to reestablish flow was imperative.

Ironically, there was no shortage of personal leakage. With my head down, feeling the pressure of Dr. K's hands trying desperately to tap the valve, I welled with tears and summoned every shred of mental strength I had to drive the repair. But mind over matter fell short as I fell apart. One straw too many. One wish too weak.

Dr. K, visibly disappointed, delivered the news with a mix of empathy and optimism, but it felt like the last ounce of my stockpiled resolve had washed away with the track of tears painted on my cheeks. Emotionally collapsed, I did my best to play the part of the sturdy survivor, but even I didn't believe my performance.

Although there was only a fraction of faith that whatever I was experiencing could be corrected without surgery, the actuality of my position was more weight than the elevator could handle. The cable snapped. Freefall into what I could only describe as an abyss. No light. No sound. An endless black hole where the aspirations of everything I dreamed I could once be descended and died. I needed a rope or a pulley because I was dropping along the line and I couldn't find a foothold. Fear thumped logic. Frustration hammered optimism. Still, the small spark in Dr. K's eyes was enough of a distant flicker to pull me from the fringe and rescue my soul.

Timing was never optimal, but this was particularly inconvenient. Constantly quenching my passion for music, I'd gotten Jess tickets for both a Broadway show and a concert later that week. I hate breaking plans and even asked Dr. K to delay any procedures until after the performances, but he wasn't willing to take chances. Looking back, I'm grateful he refused my request. Walking around the streets of New York with a malfunctioning shunt probably wasn't the best idea.

Sometimes seeing the big picture escapes me and morphs into unrealistic confidence. Sometimes it's overly grounded and crushes me under its weight. But when it comes to questioning impulsivity, experienced medical minds are normally more fitting purveyors of advice.

The surgery was scheduled, and Mom, Jess, and Joyce gathered to play the waiting game. We were under the impression that this procedure would be another valve replacement, but shortly before I was wheeled into the OR, Dr. K explained that the blockage was likely *between* the valve and the tubing. This was not my standard dysfunction. He dialed the device back up to its original setting, hoping that the removal of the debris would reestablish flow with the working valve.

Earlier in the room, I had some moments of reflection, shifting from introspection and nervous anxiety to despair and sadness. It was common to experience the full spectrum of emotions while the minutes ticked down. There was always some visceral breaking point when my perspective of the future became so bleak and shortsighted, I couldn't find any light in the tunnel. A brief stifled breakdown normally followed such revelations. But I was usually able to gather myself before the surgery started. Be strong. Be brave. Push down the fear. Hold it together for everyone else. Put on the face. Maintain. Never let them see you sweat.

The procedure went well, and Dr. K described the significant amount of debris as a kind of algae obstructing the flow in my tube. I was groggy but communicative. I revisited answers to questions I'd asked multiple times, finding it difficult to retain information. But these moments of disorientation were fairly typical for me after anesthesia. I was unaware that I was behaving unusually or having any trouble comprehending. Dazed and thoroughly confused, I only learned about my behavior from those who were lucky enough to witness my bewilderment firsthand.

Recovery time. Again. Picking up the pieces after my skull had been sliced and diced seemed to get more complicated every time. I don't know if it was age or simply my body's inability to constantly bounce back from adversity, but I felt shaken and strained. Routine CT scans said the fluid levels were finding a balance and the ventricles were slowly returning to an acceptable size. But something felt very wrong.

The nightmare of my third ventriculostomy still hung heavily in my memories. That was the last time I'd had a procedure and felt like my body was broken, regardless of what the scans had to say. That incident was enough to make me leery of positive test results eclipsing self-monitoring. It was probably a mix of equal parts gun-shyness and common sense, but I found it increasingly difficult to ignore the constant pulsations and pressure in a seemingly healthy head.

Excess blood in the ventricles acted as an irritant, and Dr. K's explanation for the palpitation was that this blood needed to work its way out of my brain and back into circulation. The thumping headaches made this waiting game less than thrilling, but I continued to trust his counsel. As much as medical technology advanced over the years, one simple fact remained unchanged: neurological surgery hijacks the body. My system was going to have to heal and recover on its own timeline, even if that meant tolerating some pain and discomfort.

Mom and Joyce drove home, and Jess stayed with me overnight. It was a testament to her nurturing nature that they felt so comfortable leaving me in her care. Jess was an incredible, unflappable source of support. There were very few people in my life that could so effortlessly handle the heavy stuff. Most friends and family tried their best to offer emotional encouragement, be a physical presence, or just empathize. These are critical aspects of the healing process, but the aptitude needed to tackle the tangled web of hospital politics and packed physician schedules took a certain gumption that was more instinctual than learned.

Jess had the perfect balance of everyday sweetness and assertive ambition. She walked the thin line between being determined and being domineering. There were moments when we literally had to stop a speeding surgeon in his tracks and insist he give us five minutes to answer a few questions. Jess always got those answers. It was difficult to avoid a negative response when playing the part of the patient's voice of concern, but she did it so magically. That sturdy backbone is what attracted me to Jess more than anything. A single mother who refused to ever bow in defeat sculpted my psyche, and that example is what helped me recognize corresponding traits in my partners. I love strong women with an agenda and a destination. Jess had that laser focus.

My lack of rebounding continued for the next few days. It became a guessing game as to why I wasn't feeling better or ready to be discharged. I couldn't seem to shake the dizziness or escalating head pressure. There was this incessant pulsing at my temples, in perfect time with my heartbeat. But instead of a calming, rhythmic patter, the pulses got louder and hammered harder every hour. Like a hostage in hospital sheets, I grew agitated and uncomfortable. There was no escape. No respite. I was caught in the waves, just riding out the storm. Feeling hurt carried with it a suitcase of burden. But helplessness trumped pain.

Walking was getting increasingly difficult. I knew staying mobile was a smart thing, but the spinning and nausea told me otherwise. I attempted short strolls in the hallway with Mom and the nurses, but even after putting my best "old man with a walker" impression on display, I was left drained and fatigued. Making headway was met with frustration, and sometimes I even felt worse as the days progressed. My healing curve had some serious gaps, and official answers were hard to find. The only constant was confusion.

Adding to the strain of the situation was Mom's attempt to stay strong and positive in the face of this hardship. She buried her sadness and stress so she could appear brave. But the weight of having to hide the heaviness wasn't healthy. The days felt so uncertain. The balance between stable confidence and complete collapse was teetering on the head of a pin, and she never wanted an emotional outburst to be the final push on the fulcrum. A mask of muscle to cloak the hurt. She would rather suffer the pain herself than let me see the internal wreckage. There was no better example of a mama lion protecting her cub.

Food was another issue. I had a regular history of dropping weight during my hospital stints, but this particular stay seemed more severe. It was never deliberate. But I don't have much of a love affair with eating in the first place. Sprinkle in some pain, nausea, and insomnia, and the idea of putting anything in my stomach loses its appeal. Unfortunately, my thin frame and high metabolism joined forces to turn skinny to skeleton. It always looked worse than it felt, but the shock factor was a lot to handle for a few of my visitors.

Getting a full meal down my throat was cause for celebration. Moms love for their sons to eat, so my resistance to adequately nourish my body was a comic push and pull that normally ended in laughter. We both realized the absurdity of a middle-aged woman trying to stuff mashed potatoes into the mouth of her grown son. It was hilarious and preposterous. But with enough fight, I usually acquiesced. It was hard to know what was best for my health when I was feeling anything but healthy.

There were more valve alterations, more X-rays, and more wondering what could possibly be happening inside my brain. Dr. K tried some aggressive adjustments to test whether my troubles were entirely pressure related or just the body's attempt to heal in a dynamic internal environment. At first, the change in pressure seemed to help with my balance and stamina, but when that momentum ended and the symptoms resurfaced, the notion of a pressure correction cure-all was dismissed. Swimming in a sea of variables, attempting to narrow the field of possibilities, was a punishing practice. It seemed even science wasn't always an exact science. It was enough to make my head spin. Pun intended.

In the middle of this hurricane of uncertainty, Dr. K said something that forever changed the trajectory of my course. During a nightly room visit, he casually mentioned that he believed a third ventriculostomy should have been successful. He felt that my condition and particular anatomy made me a perfect candidate for the procedure. Having actually looked inside my head, he was speaking from a fairly educated vantage point. He inquired about the first time it was performed and asked exactly what went wrong. I tried to be as clear and concise as possible, untying the knots within the rawness of those memories. But that incident left emotional scars that still stung. It was a dark time, and the mere mention of the episode sent me back to a pretty vulnerable space.

We were both aware of the complexity of the surgery, but the ability to eliminate the need for a shunt would certainly solve a lot of my problems. If my CSF carried excessive amounts of protein and that protein was the primary culprit responsible for the valve malfunctions, circumventing the need for a shunt altogether would be a permanent remedy. It was some heavy food for thought, but it was a meal I was in no condition to swallow at the time. I kept the idea in my back pocket and continued to watch the waves.

On the morning of my sixth day in the hospital, Dr. K came in to tell us I would be discharged. The situation wasn't improving, and he felt that just sitting in the room waiting things out didn't make much sense. He said that my healing would continue to take some patience. The brain is like a sponge and it requires fluid to function. Dr. K felt that the excess blood still needed to be absorbed by the body, and that surplus blood was what played a role in the headaches and intracranial pressure. He also mentioned that the locking stiffness in my neck was a kind of chemical meningitis. All of these ailments would improve with added rest and time, and I was asked to monitor the situation from home.

I devoted the four days before my return appointment to staying occupied and rediscovering my routine. I spent some active hours outside of the house, seeing a movie, going for walks, and testing the limits of my tolerance for movement. I certainly felt better away from the antiseptic halls and fluorescent lights of the hospital, but the pressure remained an issue. The consistent dizziness reinforced my opinion that the settings needed to be altered.

During my office visit the following Monday, Dr. K agreed to reduce the setting by 10°. He believed I would have problems if he went any lower. This was more trial and error, and the only constant marker was how I felt. I knew tweaking the levels was my only option, but it was never an arbitrary practice.

For whatever reason, modifying my valve's settings, getting consistent X-rays to verify the adjustments were correct, and waiting to see if my health improved, all seemed like perfectly normal and sane responses to what I was experiencing. Tactical and implicit, I met each step of this process with a sense of possibility that there was some magical number waiting to take all the worry away. Hanging hopes on a lotto ticket beyond my control may not have been the most efficient means of preserving morale, but it got me through the day.

Removing ideas from my head, even in their infancy, was an almost impossible task. Notions bounced off walls like a manic game of pinball, and there was nothing I could do to quiet the bells or dim the lights. I could argue it was a form of focus, but it registered more as compulsion. This propensity for cerebral hypervigilance had regularly gotten me off my ass, but it also made for an interesting romance with insomnia.

So ever since Dr. K first mentioned the idea of trying another third ventriculostomy, I couldn't stop thinking. The fact that I was extremely frustrated by my predicament helped add wind to my obsessive sails, but it was the logical core of my brain that was cognizant of the fact that all these procedures formed a queue on a definitive timeline. There was only so much the body and mind could bear. I wasn't getting younger, and each revision seemed to carry with it an extended recovery period and an entirely unfamiliar set of complications. The unpredictability of life on a wire was more than I was going to accept, so a surgery to stop all the speculation started looking like an attractive proposition.

THE PLAN

I WENT BACK to work. Everything seemed loose, like my body was disconnected from the control tower. I took each step with studied precaution, careful not to chip the porcelain and disrupt a delicate balance. With a counterfeit smile, I pretended to be normal. I greeted my tables with a version of obligatory enthusiasm and did my best to put on the show. But I was far from top form, and I'm pretty confident it read as a transparent charade. Every CT scan showed a brain in good functional shape. The levels were stable. The fluid pockets were reduced. I should have felt fine. My mind and body disagreed.

Another office visit was filled with discussions about symptoms and pressure levels. We sat in chairs and talked in circles. Indistinguishable adjectives trying to describe a measurement of health. It was all just blindfolded darts and heavy-footed ballet.

This time, we went down 10°, splitting the difference between a setting that felt almost perfect and one that felt too low. We were guessing at answers, and I was quickly losing faith in the process. The bough was breaking, weak from the weight of expectation, and a snap seemed inevitable.

I tried to stay hopeful, but there was only so much positivity I could squeeze from the stone. It felt like fighting for a front row seat in an empty theater. Besides, I was locked in the throes of targeted tunnel vision. I had one focus, one intention. I wanted a third ventriculostomy, and I wanted Dr. K to do it.

It wasn't some grand moment of inspiration, but more a lack of options that fueled my resolve. I refused to continue playing the game of endless experimentation. I wasn't getting healthier, and putting a new coat of paint on a rusty hood won't make the car any faster. I can't explain how or when I knew I reached the breaking point, but I was convinced when I found it.

There were a number of factors to consider, each one more convoluted than the next. First, the third ventriculostomy would not be deemed medically necessary. I was technically in good health, and the scans and office follow-ups were paper trail proof of that. Convincing an insurance company to cover an expensive, risky procedure is a challenge in its own right. Persuading them to foot the bill for a healthy individual who just underwent a surgery for the exact same condition was a different obstacle altogether. Factor in the potential snags with my medical coverage and I was standing at the base of a steep mountain.

Making the decision to present my proposal to Dr. K was both frightening and exhilarating. For the first time in my life, I was taking ownership of my medical needs. In my refusal to follow the plotted course, I was lighting a new trail. But without markers or guideposts, I knew the finish line would be hard to find. Plus, if I encountered some reluctance or even an outright denial on his part, I would be shattered.

I chose to meet with him alone. These were the seeds of my strategy, and I needed to accept the responsibility and the consequences. I knew Mom would ultimately support whatever choice I made, but I didn't want anyone else in the office diverting his attention during my pitch. There was way too much weight hanging in the balance of what I was about to say, and I needed to go inside myself for that final push. Also, I wanted Dr. K's sole focus. I had to look into his eyes to deliver my plea. He had a product I was desperate to buy. He could play the savior and I could be the saved. In its most basic form, this was a conversation about a transaction between two men.

He greeted me as an equal, without status or pretension. He didn't cram our conversation between medical rounds or bites of egg salad. He took the time and gave me the attention that I envisioned but never expected. We sat in his office without barriers, and we left preconceptions at the door. He appeared as eager to hear what I had to say as I was to report it. After such diligent planning, it was surprisingly effortless. That immediate comfort level I first found with him became the backbone of our interaction.

I can't say it felt like speaking with an old friend. We weren't there yet. But the flowing ease of our exchange helped replace the butterflies with steady earnestness. I was able to focus on the task at hand instead of being reminded of the pit in my stomach. My defenses were armed, anticipating some resistance, but he agreed almost instantly that something had to be done to correct my condition. Since he was the original proponent of the procedure, it didn't take long for us to settle on a solution. However, the agreement to venture down that road didn't come without stipulations.

There were still some lists left to check and some knots to unwind before we could assign a definite date. He understood the issues with the insurance company, but promised me he would do everything in his power to ensure coverage. The only red tape would be framing the procedure as medically necessary, but Dr. K believed that quality of life was as much a factor in this decision as physical health. Plus, the more procedures I had to tolerate, the greater the chance for complications and future medical hardships. Some extra costs now could save countless dollars down the road.

He also explained that he would be bringing in another surgeon to assist. He wanted someone with even greater endoscopic experience, particularly because the level of difficulty involved with the procedure allowed very little room for error. I offered no objections. I didn't care if it took an army of the most brilliant minds the medical field could produce. My only request was that there would be no mistakes this time. The aftermath of the previous attempt was still fresh in my memories, and this was fast feeling like my last real shot at an actual solution.

I wholeheartedly put my faith and trust in one man's hands. I did this because I felt it was right. I did this because I knew he believed me and believed in me. I was willing to lay all my cards on the table and follow the hunch that this person could change the course of my life. There are very few moments when we are positive the actions we take will undoubtedly achieve extraordinary results. This was that moment.

Dr. K also asked that I see a therapist regularly during the months leading up to my procedure. He was adamant about me clearing the fog in my head to be absolutely certain that what I was about to endure was coming from a place of lucid, conscious thought. He didn't want my decision to be a reaction to the frustrations of my past but a levelheaded step into a healthier future. I was well aware that delving into my subconscious was probably going to dig up a lot more than some hesitations about the hospital. There was ample fodder for a trained psychologist, and I knew she would have a field day with my complicated history and many neuroses. But hey, maybe it was time to clean my closet a little. Two birds, one big boulder.

We met with the assisting surgeon, Dr. G, and he discussed the procedure in greater detail. Having had a bit more experience, he was able to clearly describe what results we could expect following a successful third ventriculostomy. He was calm and thorough and shared some similarities in personality with Dr. K. Integrating complementary individual skill sets, they seemed like a perfect fit and a perfect team. I still felt like I was walking into the flames, but two talented firemen were there to handle the heat.

Insurance concerns remained a factor, and Dr. G wasn't in my network of participating surgeons. But he assured us that it wouldn't be an issue. He was willing to waive the standard compensation for his services, choosing instead to direct his focus on effectively completing the procedure. It was just another example of the extraordinary character and integrity he displayed throughout this process.

With some of the worry out of the way, I turned my attention to the therapy sessions. Scaring the skeletons into the light, while more thoroughly scrutinizing the potentially dark tunnel ahead, became my next emotional obstacle course. Having consistently shunned any serious attempts at counseling, this was basic training and I knew I'd be sore from the effort. But I was dedicated to carrying out Dr. K's wishes, and this was a major part of the preparation.

I wasn't entirely sure what to expect when I arrived at the office of Dr. W. She was a friendly woman in her mid-forties who welcomed me with an open, understanding posture. The salubrious space felt more like a living room, fully lending itself to the torrent of personal disclosures cascading from her patients. She was a mother, with a clan of crying children at her feet. She was there to nod supportively and wipe the noses and bandage the knees of the weak-willed, melodramatic masses too incapable of working through their own issues. She could posit theories or explanations as to why they were struggling for attention, drowning in feelings of inadequacy, or resenting their parents for not showing them enough attention. They would sit there for an hour every week and gush about everything from their inability to maintain a relationship to the reasons they weren't being promoted at work. She could pat them on the head, reassure them that things would change with a little more effort, and collect her checks. She was a huckster selling miracle tonic at a road show disguised as a haven for better health. Or at least that's what I thought before I joined the club.

The idea behind the sessions was to clear my head of any psychological residue that might affect my decision to willingly undergo an "elective" procedure. In no way did I feel like there was even a choice on the table, but technically speaking, I wasn't in any desperate need of surgical correction. Because of the risks involved and the possible physical and mental repercussions following an operation of this difficulty, Dr. K wanted me to enter the OR with an easy mind and an unencumbered conscience, regardless of the potential dangers ahead.

Grabbing a shovel and digging through the backlog of buried emotions proved less difficult than I'd imagined. The sessions quickly evolved from guarded chats to friendly, organic disclosures. Dr. W had an easy, free-flowing style that partnered well with my readiness to share. As any good therapist trained in psychology was prone to do, she allowed me to arrive at conclusions and discoveries at my own pace. I was made to feel like I was constructing some great, mysterious puzzle and every found piece was a new victory. Because of my wariness to believe the expertise of strangers, this was probably the only way I would have been able to accept such revelations. I was very good at buying what I was selling.

Our departure from anything surgery related and our journey into my cluttered closet of repressed anger, unhealed abandonment wounds, and my overcompensation in the face of astonishingly low self-esteem provided countless hours of psyche-unraveling fun. I won't say that she was a one-upper, but there were some moments when I felt like she was offering me examples that felt oddly competitive. I was happy to relinquish the trophy for the most emotional hardships. That was a race I did not need to win.

Gaining a grip on some of the shackles that weighed me down for years and understanding that there were tools I could use to open a few of the locks were insightful and valuable experiences. Even while I was in the middle of the sessions, I was able to take a step back and recognize the usefulness in her methodology. Greater mental clarity and a deeper understanding of the motivations behind certain actions in life are gifts that far too few get the opportunity to receive. I will be forever grateful to have been given the introductory course.

The strain on my relationship with Jess was another story. The fact that I never fully recovered from the last revision, coupled with the daunting prospects of what was waiting in the wings, left little room or energy for cultivating a successful, mutually rewarding union. It was an unfortunate casualty of war. She was immensely supportive and an unshakable nurturer, but my head was figuratively and literally whirling. I simply didn't have the energy or the determination to add another spinning plate to my act. I was sorry for our breakup, but my head and my heart each had their own, separate agenda.

The preparation continued. It became nearly impossible for me to think of anything else. I wandered through my workdays, doing my best impression of a stable, balanced waiter. I greeted each table with featherweight shoulders and a porcelain grin. I wore a mask of confidence and focused on steadying my trays, keeping one foot in front of the other. My disposition was airy, and the conversations stayed loosely light. Every action was a secret I wished I didn't have to keep. No one knew what lived behind the smile.

As the surgery date neared, the requisite jitters came with a small surge of doubt for the first time since my office proposal to Dr. K. I guess that was expected. The ducks can all sit neatly lined in rows, but the sight of an oncoming wave will make even the steadiest bird shake. I knew what I wanted. I knew the costs and the risks. I wasn't deviating from the charted course, but for some reason, a heavier dose of the potential ramifications took residence in my head. One of the smartest things I've ever done was fight that impulse to waver. Deciphering between an instinctual fight-or-flight reaction and a case of cold feet was not always simple. But this was a situation where nerves were merely nerves.

THE MAIN EVENT

AFTER CONSIDERABLE THOUGHT and rumination, my insurance company authorized the procedure and a date was set. Dr. K's assistant was wonderfully instrumental in making sure the proper steps were taken to secure approval. Without access behind the curtain, we were often left waiting for a phone to ring, trying to preserve some shred of sanity. We didn't know if the insurance company was putting up a fight, flatly refusing, or charitably accepting the idea. It wasn't until we heard the full story that we learned the last part of the authorization process took less than forty-five minutes. We subjected ourselves to unhealthy levels of stress simply due to a lack of information.

From office visits to routine exams to lengthy hospital stays, one of the most unfortunate aspects of this ordeal was the regularly unavoidable frustration we faced with gaps in the transmission chain. I understand it would be nearly impossible to relay every piece of pertinent news, but a better system of providing crucial updates would smooth some of the miscommunication wrinkles and probably lower the blood pressure and panic levels of the patients. Of course, that might make the medical experience less complicated and more linear. No one wants something crazy like that.

I arrived at Northern Westchester two days before the scheduled surgery. My valve was dialed down to a level that would most effectively inhibit CSF flow. Basically, it was a deliberate attempt to make the shunt system fail. The brain's ventricles needed to be plump with fluid for a third ventriculostomy to even be attempted. Luckily, the programmable valve lent itself well to that manipulation. Again, it took several attempts to achieve the correct setting, but the X-rays confirmed the adjustment was made. So I went back upstairs to my room and eagerly waited for my malfunction.

Mom made the obligatory family phone calls; I talked to some friends, read some magazines, and tried to mentally prepare myself for the approaching tornado. Throughout my history, a clogged valve or a flooded ventricle came as a surprise. Normally, the timing was less than ideal and my life screeched to a halt. I had to quickly evaluate the optimum way to handle the problem, find the necessary medical assistance, and plan for a lengthy forced vacation. This was the unique case where I knew what was going to happen to me, and I actually *wanted* it to occur. I had some trouble wrapping my head around this concept because I'd been so conditioned to regard a shunt malfunction as code red. Now, the troops readied themselves at the door of the plane, but I never gave the order to jump.

Aside from the psychological confusion, certain moments couldn't have felt more familiar. The building intracranial pressure started slowly, but soon the waves were rocking the shores of my skull with every movement of my neck. Bending down to pick something up was out of the question. Nodding or shaking my head would amplify the waves, and I'd have to wait for the brief vision blackouts to subside. Still, sitting in the safety of the hospital environment lessened some of the usual anxiety and I was able to more readily relax into the reality of my position.

Thinking my way out of the monster's lair was a weapon I'd wielded many times over the course of this affliction. The success of that strategy cemented my theory that manipulating the mind can, at certain times, be used to trump the body's physical ailments. There were circumstances and levels of pain when this method proved ineffective. But several moments of discomfort were left defenseless against my clever mind meld. I was Spock of the neuroscience wing.

In the morning, transport arrived to take me for a CT scan. Our hope was that the ventricles had increased enough to support the adjustment. Ironically, I was feeling pretty good, and this was the one time we wanted the symptoms to be more severe than pleasant. But sometimes indicators like headaches or dizziness didn't demonstrate a direct correlation between what was happening on the inside and outside of the brain. The scans told the real story.

I spoke to the nurse and Dr. K briefly, and he confirmed the ventricles had increased considerably in size. He was pleased with the results, and he saw no reason to deviate from our original timeline. I took some extra laps around the hallway to stretch my legs, open my lungs, and focus my thoughts. This was it. All lights were green. By my own will, I was walking into the heart of the hurricane. Time to stare down the storm and see who blinks.

It was a difficult night, as were most nights before my procedures. My head swam with thoughts of hope, fused with flashes of regret. This was the first time I had *chosen* to be there. The emergency swelling was induced by my own request. I was in a dangerous position because I asked for it. It was a strike out or grand slam moment, and I fully understood the consequences of my decisions.

Human nature offers the option to run when danger is near. It is only when the attainment of seemingly impossible gains suddenly seems possible that we ignore that instinct for flight. However, I could feel victory and defeat in equal doses, so any definitive action remained unlikely.

I eventually drifted into a light sleep until the pharmaceutical sounds of daylight replaced the uneasiness of a long nervous night. A nurse arrived to draw blood and start an IV. To my utter lack of astonishment, she was unable to establish a drip. My fickle thick skin was the last thing I needed to think about that early in the morning, but I knew the IV team would come to the rescue as they had done so many times in the past.

A quiet, reflective aura settled over the room. Mom and I were thumbing through books and magazines, searching for distraction. Our thoughts were too mercurial to vocalize, so we sat in silent contemplation. It was the culmination of what felt like a lifetime's worth of worry and it all came down to one moment, one last stretch for that elusive ring. My heart was pounding, and the panic of all that was waiting for me felt like some slow, conscious burial beneath an avalanche of sand. The transition from fully commanding my journey to this absolute lack of control was suffocating.

Some small talk just before my transport team arrived helped shave off the top layer of nerves. We shared empty commentary about the articles we were reading. Sometimes just breaking the ice allowed more oxygen into the air. Stress levels were peaking, and I'm sure my blood pressure was paying the price. I allowed myself to obsess about the IV placement and whether or not the flow was sufficient. Obviously, a nurse or the anesthesiologist would have corrected any issue, but whatever I could use as an excuse was a welcome diversion.

I was taken to the holding area just outside of the OR, and I had my last opportunity to speak with Dr. K and Dr. G before the surgery. I tried to make my appeal for an aggressive execution. I'd carried with me the nagging suspicion that my last third ventriculostomy failed due to a lack of sufficient perforation of the blocked ventricular wall. Even when it was explained that the complexity of the procedure could have yielded a number of imperfect results, my fears and regrets were never assuaged, despite the proposed logic. I also made a request for the complete removal of my existing shunt. I had concerns that any CSF leaking into the valve, regardless of the lowered setting, might offset some vital flow through the fresh opening. Plus, it felt like the evacuation of all synthetic material from my body would be the final step in eliminating every memory of this prolonged struggle with an unpredictable, defective anatomy.

Unfortunately, my surgical team had other ideas. They explained that even though my valve and tubing had been removed during the previous attempt at this procedure, it was not the safest option. The existing shunt could function as an emergency escape route should the newly formed opening close or become clogged with debris. The CSF would theoretically find its way back to the valve and my doctor could dial up the settings to reactivate the shunt's operation. This was not at all what I wanted to hear, but they promised that after six months to a year of excellent performance and overall health, the entire shunt system could be extracted during a simple office procedure. I reluctantly accepted the news and put my trust in their competence and experience.

Watching these two men at my bedside, a rush of anxiety came over me. Like the final seconds before a gunshot begins the race, my angst and nerves twisted together in a cocktail of stifling panic. I had one final opportunity to pull the plug and walk away. I had one more chance to admit I'd made a terrible mistake and march out of that hospital holding on to at least a small prospect of manageable health. I could run away from the complicated risks and wait for some safer future technology to glue the broken pieces. This was my life in the balance, and a life of struggle and heartbreak was better than no life at all.

Dr. K saw this shift and looked me squarely in the eyes. He reassured me that this was all my decision and I could choose to continue or stop. The fact that he recognized my reluctance cleared some of the haze and refocused my attention. He cared about me as a suffering individual. He cared about me as a person. I was a special case. I was not a patient ID number or some appointment on his list. I never was. It was the reason I chose him in the first place, and it was the reason I decided to let go of any more foot-dragging and self-sabotage. I nodded in simple agreement and finally allowed myself a release from the chains.

The anesthesiologist assistant stayed with us for a little while, and this simple thoughtful action helped calm my nerves. I needed to breathe, and I needed perspective. My blood pressure was steadily climbing, and my weight had plummeted since my last stay. The stress and strain of walking through life on a balance beam had taken its toll. Any gesture or moment that could disconnect me from my erratic brain and put me back in my body was a welcome reprieve from the routine chaos. I was grateful for the company and kind words.

The time had come to make that final push into the OR. I said my goodbyes through apprehensive eyes and, for the very first time, grasped the concept of finality. Through each of my previous surgeries, I understood the notion of risks and complications, but I processed them as remote improbabilities. Now, as I watched the image of Mom grow smaller and smaller with every passing ceiling tile, I felt the heaviness of irrevocability. There was just something more potent and visceral about that moment. I couldn't clearly distinguish between a forecast of tragedy or triumph, but I knew the results would be conclusive.

My gut never failed me before, and now it was predicting an epic final showdown. The universe had the ball in its court, but I knew my surgeons were ready to play. I crossed my fingers and toes, felt the warm sting of drugs pass through my IV, and consciously closed my eyes for possibly the last time.

Mom sat in the waiting area, holding her breath and counting the minutes. Even though no specific time frame had been given, she believed it might take about two hours to complete the ventriculostomy. She watched the various patients shuttle down winding hallways in wheelchairs or on stretchers and thought about their worries, their fears, their histories. She wondered how many times they'd seen these sterile white walls and dreamed of a day when they would forget the smell of warm hospital food trays and the early-morning buzz of blood pressure monitors.

Almost every patient comes attached with a family or loved one who is subjected to the same suffering and desperation. Many times, those at the bedside bear much more of the burden. The sick are often sedated, medicated, or too weak to stay awake. Their healthy visitors are left enduring the weight of information and perspective. They are the ears that have to process the bad news. They are the heavy hearts and slumped shoulders that must internalize the fears and poor odds. They are the smiling faces masking doubt and disappointment. They are the insomniacs who can hear the footsteps of an approaching surgeon thirty feet before they walk in the door. They are the foundation, and without them, the structure would fall.

Mom epitomized this position, and I would have crumbled under the weight of that unshakable strain years earlier if I had been forced to tackle even a day of this alone. There is no act or sum of money that could come close to repaying that debt. She was my protector, my crutch, and my savior.

As the minutes mounted, her nerves followed suit. She had never been cool and calm in a crisis, and this was basically a quiet emergency taking place inside the prison of her speculation. No one was there to offer reassurance or help her find some perspective. She sat alone with her journal and her agony. I can't imagine constantly having to fight that war without reinforcements. But she was built for battle, and this was simply another day in the trenches. Wringing her hands, she scanned the room for answers and tried to visualize a happy ending. Then, Dr. K walked over to her chair and asked to have a word.

She studied his face for some type of verdict as he broke into a gentle, reassuring smile. The procedure was a perfect success. The perforation in the ventricular wall was established and the CSF surged into the newly constructed opening. The fluid fled to the fresh real estate like a scene from some 1890s land rush documentary. My surgeons were able to watch the results live, the true test of a successful penetration. The outcome was so positive, Dr. K remarked that (had a camera been in the OR) the video could have been used to teach medical students the optimal way to establish CSF flow during a third ventriculostomy.

To say that Mom was happy with the news would be an understatement of laughable proportions. There was no greater strain than knowing her child was in jeopardy. There was no greater relief than knowing he was safe. The universe reached down and lifted the extra tonnage from her shoulders. Pounds of heartache and stress fell away, almost magically. All the tension carried on her face disappeared. It was an instantaneous transformation. Mom was able to take a deep breath and stand up straight for the first time in a long while.

Only ten staples. A small horseshoe incision on the right side of my head was all the remaining evidence of the medical miracle that had taken place. I was brought to recovery and was able to answer correctly all the basic questions to test proper brain function. What was my name? What year was it? Who was the president? I know that seems simple, but there were times when those queries felt like an interrogation in some "Final Jeopardy!" round, so I was relieved to be coherent. But I did ask the nurses and Mom what had been done, if the surgery was successful, if the shunt had been removed, etc., so maybe I was slightly less lucid than I appeared. Either way, I was grateful to be alive and tried to put the pieces together as I took in the surroundings of the room.

Regardless of any surgery's success, the first night in the ICU is never easy. Constant achiness, soreness around the wound site, and a throbbing headache was par for the course. Add this to the fact that I had to constantly battle the nurses about standing to pee (when they wanted me to remain in bed) and it made for a pretty lengthy evening. But there was always the dawn. I waited for that first crack in the curtains with the anticipation of a puppy in a pet store.

I started getting a little concerned about the headache and low-grade fever, but Dr. K assured me the scans looked good and the body was probably just absorbing some blood from the procedure. I normally don't respond to mild pain meds, and the heavy stuff made me too nauseous. Usually, I'd just grind through the discomfort and wait for it to pass. As long as I could reconcile the fact that everything was okay inside my head, I was generally fine navigating the rough waters.

There was a timeless quality to life in a hospital room. The hours seemed to tick away at a snail's pace, and then, all of a sudden, the day was done. Random bits of television sound bites and flashes of scurrying hospital staff chasing monitors sounding alarms blended together to form this cacophony of randomness. It became a kind of white noise that grew more arbitrary the longer I was bathing in it.

People who live near airports stop hearing the planes. The sound of life begins to drown out the sound of thought. Maybe that's a good thing in a hospital. When you're stuck beneath crisply tucked sheets with nothing but time on your hands, too much thought can be dangerous.

By the next morning, the headache had become too intense to ignore. It was unrelenting and the reassurance of healthy scans wasn't pacifying the pain. Dr. K had another theory, and it made a lot of sense. My brain was now experiencing a low-pressure CSF flow, whereas the shunt generated a medium flow. That slight variation could have been enough to throw my carefully calibrated system for a curve. The fact that he came to the hospital from home to deliver the news in person was further proof of his constant willingness to alleviate our concerns.

That night, the throbbing hit some pretty unbearable heights, so I began a Tylenol regimen every four hours. The pulsing in my temples seemed to retreat a little, and I was able to get some sleep. Sometimes even the slightest comfort cushion did wonders for my psyche. Everything was relative. The same amount of pain in another context would have caused exponentially more concern. But since I'd battled pounding like this for so long, any respite felt like a gift. I was grateful for the relief.

The next morning, Dr. K asked if I thought I was ready to leave or if I felt I should wait another day. He was leaning toward the latter, and I agreed. Mom and I took our routine laps around the neuroscience wing. I was able to recycle a tired joke I used every time we made these sluggish strolls by sitting down at the piano in the game room and playing the same simple song. The laughs never got old for me. For Mom, it was probably a different story. But I found my smiles wherever I could.

Maintaining a level of perspective was crucial. Even though my body was rattled from the attack, everything I hoped would happen had come to fruition. The reports and scans were stellar, my surgeons were overjoyed, and I was feeling more energy each day. Allowing my system the time it needed to recover and finding comfort in the notion that I was healthy were sometimes easier intended than done. I knew I had to let myself adjust to all these changes and discover the balance required to thrive. But those days were long, and patience ran thin in the middle of that process.

Dr. K came in the next day to give me my official discharge. There was a flurry of thoughts and emotions running through my head, and I did my best to make sense of everything. Being told it was time to leave the hospital meant I was no longer in a state where I needed immediate care. But it was also a harsh reminder that I was going to have to live outside the safety of an institution specifically designed to keep me protected.

Normally, this wasn't much of a consideration. In the past, I was glad to go home and return to reality. But I think there was, invariably, a nagging curiosity about when I would find myself in the same predicament again. This time I was all in, so the idea that something could bring me back to the starting line was terrifying. If this failed, after being performed to perfection, what did that say about my future, my life? That would be my second unsuccessful third ventriculostomy. Add to that five different surgeries for shunt implantations or revisions and the odds of me finding a workable solution to this condition seemed pretty bleak. Seven brain surgeries in eleven years, six of them in a six-year block. It was enough to drive even the most optimistic mind a little mad.

THE COURAGE

THE UPS AND downs of the healing process continued to be both promising and unpredictable. With each procedure, my body was a little less quick to bounce back, and this was no exception. There was an overwhelming sense of hope, but that optimism was countered by my pragmatic nature. I wanted this to be the solution to a long line of disappointments. I wanted to feel like I could take on the challenges of the world with a comparable set of tools, unhindered by this chain of weak links. I wanted to feel confident in my abilities and myself. I wanted to live.

Some days the headaches were there. Some days they were gone. The area around the wound was sore, and there were occasional pressure fluctuations. I could tell my body was trying to figure out its new pipeline. The dizziness would creep in unexpectedly, and sometimes reading or watching any kind of video proved impossible.

There was also this new pulling sensation on the right side of my head that felt like little ropes with grappling hooks dragging at the insides of my skull. Many of the discomforts were familiar territory. This one was unique. It was sporadic but uncomfortable. I had to understand that everything I thought I knew about my brain had changed. There was going to be some very unfamiliar territory ahead.

Little by little, I started to find my strength, and my balance improved. Five days after I was discharged, I had an appointment with Dr. K to get my staples removed. The staples always sting when they're extracted, but it was nice to see the horseshoe scar without its additional "bling." He was pleased with my progress and the fact that I was feeling better so quickly. He believed that was a major sign the ventriculostomy was working. The radiology reports showed a significant decrease in the size of my ventricles, and Dr. K said I could return to work whenever I felt ready.

I met with Dr. G about ten days later. I still felt okay, but I wasn't doing quite as well. The constant swings kept me on my toes, but they also added an extra edge of worry I wish I didn't have to entertain during that unpredictable time. Still, seeing Dr. G and his reassuring smile was such a gift. I somehow managed to find two genius surgeons who were as kind and gentle as Buddhist monks. It was astounding. To be that evolved mentally and emotionally was an anomaly of nature. They were the closest examples of super-humans that I'd ever known.

I also gained some important pieces of information from the visit. He explained that it could take anywhere from six to twelve weeks for the body to fully acclimatize to the changes. He also mentioned that there was debris present at the tip of the remaining shunt's catheter, which could eventually prevent all fluid from passing in or out of the tubing.

Oddly, the more clogged the catheter became, the more fluid was forced through the ventriculostomy's opening. So an impacted catheter was not necessarily a bad thing. Still, should I choose to have the shunt removed, he recommended waiting six months to a year. There was never a reason to disturb the brain's habitat unless it was completely necessary. If the shunt wasn't causing some kind of problem, the removal would be more elective than imperative. It had always been my wish to complete the process by evicting all artificial "squatters" from my body. But, apparently, I needed to wait a while.

Getting back to work at the restaurant wasn't as easy as expected. The stress of waiting tables, extensive time spent on my feet, and the hot, humid summer didn't help. I was beginning to question whether

I had returned too soon. I'd spent a large chunk of my life quickly rebounding from these surgeries, but this was a new game with new rules. My self-assigned invincibility as a man with an unpredictable shunt no longer applied. My head was still solving the riddles posed by the third ventriculostomy and I wasn't listening. Most days were spent battling headaches or dizziness, and that was not the best fight to have while stuck in the throes of the service industry.

I continued my sessions with Dr. W. Even though our discussions were originally intended to mentally prepare me for the surgery, we detoured from that subject matter pretty early in the process. We jumped into my childhood, the rationale behind the way I interacted with the world, and how the consistent surgeries had affected my ability to find any sense of peace or security. We also spent a significant amount of time on my reactions to Paul's death earlier that spring.

Two months before I was wheeled into the operating room, I walked into a funeral home to see an emaciated version of a man I vaguely remembered. I went to support my family and to find some sense of closure. Neither happened. I hadn't seen my estranged father since that first surgery eleven years earlier, but there is an inexpressible vacancy left when a parent dies, regardless of the circumstances.

There was still a lot to explore, and I wanted to make more sense of everything that had happened, both from an emotional and intellectual perspective. She was very helpful in facilitating that clarity, and I was grateful for her guidance. Achieving some form of mental and physical equilibrium during a time of significant trauma takes an army. But I had some well-trained troops.

Another colossal concern on my plate was my impending move to Los Angeles. Originally, I wanted to take the trip in August, about nine months after I returned to Newburgh from Buffalo. Obviously, two unexpected brain surgeries derailed that agenda. But in place of a timely departure, I was given the hope of stable health. If I had left earlier, I would have battled those same roadblocks in a far less forgiving environment. The challenges could have been severe enough to send me back home. Now, it was time to make some phone calls and finish planning my new life.

Apprehensions played games with my resolutions, but I tried to separate the fear of falling into further health problems from the fear of leaving the safety net. Both were valid concerns, but the former played on my control issues while the latter came from a space of genuine worry. The brain was wired to find solace in comfort and routine. After standing at death's door more times than I wanted to count, I realized there was always one constant. I wasn't alone.

When I stepped out of the shower at thirteen after watching those little men rappelling down the shampoo bottles, when I was falling asleep in the car on the way to the hospital in New York because my brain was shutting down, when campus police took me to the health center because I was too delusional to think for myself, when I woke up to a pillow drenched in CSF from a leaking head wound, when I decided I had undergone enough and I was ready to throw in the towel, when I fought through blinding pressure and dizziness during visits from my college friends, when I broke down in tears trying to get a baseball cap over an axe-sized gash, when I couldn't wrap my mind around the fact that a valve had stopped working again, and when I was told the exceptional news of a picture-perfect procedure…Mom was there.

The notion that I would leave the one grounded force in my world for a fresh start on the other side of the country seemed certifiable. But there was something that was drawing me to the West Coast. I guess it was a persistent sense that I was missing everything and everyone else I wanted in my life. I felt like a native from the first minute I stepped foot on LA soil, so there was this magnetic pull for me to return home. I wasn't sure exactly what that meant or where I would ultimately land, but I knew the core group of friends I had established could lay a solid foundation to let me explore. The first step of the journey was strategy. It was time to call Eric.

Asking your friend to take a week off work, fly home to New Jersey, drive with you across America, and set up temporary living quarters in his shared house were lofty requests. But Eric was the connector in our group. He was the hub of our collective wheel. Everyone knew him, and everyone liked him. He even maintained college friendships that the rest of us abandoned years earlier. He was a born leader, organizer, and planner. I'd allowed him to take the reigns of our adventures for as long as I could remember. This was no exception. However, I was aware of the distance, and I wasn't blind to the fact that this request would be a significant disruption of a life he was in the process of building. Still, he was my closest friend, and he knew exactly what it took for me to get to this point. He was there through all the mud and muck, and he understood my desire to finally join the family.

We began our standard routine of returning missed phone calls and trying to negotiate contrasting time zones and fluctuating work schedules. When we were able to have a lengthy discussion, the itinerary came together fairly quickly. Eric was going to fly home with his girlfriend to spend a few days with his family. She would then fly back to LA, and I would pick him up in a Jeep loaded to the gills with boxes and belief.

It seemed pretty straightforward. We were slated to push off in mid-November, so that left me with less than three months to tie up any loose ends, continue to heal, and gain the courage I needed to say goodbye to safety. It was incredible how quickly the days disappeared once the sands in the hourglass started to fall. The countdown was on, and I had a long checklist to follow. I decided I would approach this challenge like all the rest. One foot in front of the other.

That period turned out to be a very special time in my life. The restaurant was undergoing a change in ownership, so my shifts were limited while they started construction and some light remodeling. I wasn't complaining. I still felt my worst at work. Besides, I'd already saved the money I needed to buy my Jeep, plus a little cushion to get me started in a new city without a job.

Mom and I took full advantage of the days we had left together. We built a strategy to tackle the task of transporting a life from one side of the country to the other. My obsessive need to back up and catalog all my music and writing was met with understanding smiles. Our car shopping adventures were filled with comedy. We always found silliness in the most mundane activities. The simple times were the happiest times. I shared my concerns and excitements, and she was there to offer guidance and help calm my nerves. We both understood the enormity of my decision, but our conversations weren't weighed down by the inevitable departure date. Without consciously saying anything to drive our communication in a specific direction, we simply embraced the moments. We couldn't have built a better runway for my launch.

I began the daunting task of boxing my life. Or more specifically, boxing the maximum amount of life that could fit into a Jeep, without it looking like a target for thieves at every hotel stop. This whole process required a series of agonizing decisions. I had to seriously consider the fact that I was moving into a house full of friends who already had plenty of stuff in their storage. The last thing I wanted was to be a burden. They were exhibiting an incredible level of generosity and understanding by allowing me into their space. I didn't need to become an uninvited thorn in the paw.

What originally seemed like ample time to draw up my blueprint soon became a race to the finish as the months melted away. I said my goodbyes to family, grasping the reality that I may not see them again for a long time. I've never been very good at emotional projection, normally living in the present moment as opposed to thinking about how my specific actions might affect the big picture. But when I saw Joyce's eyes well up with tears the morning before she headed back home to Connecticut, even I understood the significance of what was about to take place. This wasn't temporary. I wasn't blindly throwing darts at some unattainable dream. This was my new real life.

The time had finally come to leave. Just as I had done in the fall of my junior year, I sat in a car stuffed with everything I needed to face this next chapter in California. Again, I was bound for New Jersey to pick up my traveling companion. The rules had been revised. We were young adults with lives of our own creation. We weren't driving west with wide eyes and the naiveté that comes from the unstructured track of youth. We were ready to make our way in a town that always felt right.

The end goal may have changed, but the friendship and support were constant. No matter the time or the miles, Eric and I always fell back into our patterns. It was a unique choreography that came from the combination of years spent together and an inherent, shared like-mindedness. This was almost impossible to explain to those who never understood it.

There was very little fear the first time I made this pilgrimage. If anything, I was defiant. I chose to spit in the face of my condition by braving uncharted waters without a lifeboat. I had to prove to myself that I wasn't going to be a victim of my unpredictable body. Honestly, it was probably nothing more than dumb luck that something didn't happen during that semester. Part of me understood it was foolish to live without medical contacts or safety nets. But an even bigger part of me had to do it.

Now, I was a little older, a little wiser, and I had a lot more at stake. The internship program was simply a notion of my independence. The third ventriculostomy was the reason I could legitimately exercise it. This was a gift given to me by fate and timing, and I wasn't going to allow anything to destroy that. I was more than grateful, for so many people who were willing to help me heal the hurt. My physical brain, as well as what was going on inside of it, had been through hell and back. I was finally free of the unpredictable tether that constantly found a way to snap me back to the starting line. After a long reluctance to move, I was ready to run on my own terms.

Thought and execution are two very different animals. Although I had set my mind on this mission, there was still an incredible amount of apprehension racing through my veins. I was looking out of the cargo bay of the plane, parachute attached. I saw a revitalizing world waiting for me to take that leap. But I saw Mom with a nervous smile, and I saw what happens when the parachute doesn't open. I saw myself flying through the clouds, invigorated by the thrill of freedom. I watched her image get smaller and smaller the farther I fell.

I was leaving everything I knew and racing toward the uncertain possibility of a chance to swim without shackles. It was a leap of faith in the purest sense of the expression. So I summoned every ounce of strength I had and I started the Jeep. I knew what I was doing, and it tore every single fiber of my heart from its casing. I watched Mom get smaller and smaller in the rearview mirror as I traveled up the street. Every instinct said to stop. But I kept my foot on the gas and set out for the Garden State.

Eric's childhood home wasn't exactly in my backyard. It took some time to travel to South Jersey, and I spent the hours processing all that had just taken place. It felt lonely to be driving away from my security and barreling toward the unknown, but I was confident that seeing Eric would help ease my mind and reassure me I was doing the right thing.

There were some radical differences in the atmosphere of his house, compared to those pre-internship preparations. This time, I didn't walk into a packing storm of boxes and papers and last-minute strategies. I didn't witness Eric and his family in full attack mode, making sure every last detail was in place. Things were much more relaxed, calmer. Although, there was still a little of that quintessential energy and humor that only Eric's clan could provide.

Just as we had done the last time, our first destination was the house of Eric's uncle in Cincinnati. It was a perfect resting stop, but it was enough of a drive to feel like we accomplished something. His uncle was a warm, intelligent man with a peaceful spirit. We brought in a few things from the Jeep and intended to crash pretty early. But sometimes the road to insomnia is paved with good intentions.

I was a mess. As soon as I put my head down on the pillow, my brain went into anxiety overdrive. Suddenly, doubts and fears and regrets flooded my mind. I felt like I was strapped to a neurotic locomotive racing down an abandoned track. Everything felt wrong. I thought I made the worst possible decision. I didn't know what I was doing, why I had left so early, or how I was supposed to simply transplant myself to the other side of the country and hope everything would be fine. It seemed insane. It seemed idiotic. I had to tell Eric the truth. I needed to go back.

The sleepless night turned into morning, and I was paralyzed. Smiling and greeting Eric and his uncle with jovial small talk had all the ingredients of a clumsy performance. They must have known something was terribly wrong. If they did, they were nice enough not to expose my fragile state.

I felt caged, pinned to the wall, and wanted desperately to disappear. It wasn't just my feelings at play. Eric had made a commitment to do this with me. He was losing work and money and time he could have spent pursuing his goals in LA. How could I just deliver the news that he should probably buy a plane ticket and have his uncle take him over to Cincinnati International?

The stakes were too high. This also meant abandoning my dreams, sliding back into a cocoon of the familiar, and saying goodbye to any chance of sustaining relationships with my best friends in the world. It would be raising the white flag and admitting that an unseen enemy would forever dictate my life. This admission was damning and definite. There would not be another chance, not this way. It was fundamentally fight or flight, and I was put to the most primal test.

I found a quiet spot outside, and I called Mom in a panic. This was probably the last thing she wanted or needed to hear, but we'd made a life of unfavorable situations and terrifying phone conversations, so this really wasn't anything new. I voiced my concerns and tried to hold back tears as I described my trepidation. She remained calm and assured me she would support whatever decision I made. She was aware of what derailing my plans might mean, but she was more levelheaded than I was about the demolition of any future prospects or possibilities. She felt that if my body and brain were having this significant reaction, it might be wise to listen to my gut instinct. Still, she thought I would be fine if I chose to continue on my path.

I was instantly comforted, but I wasn't any closer to a resolution. If I decided to carry on, I could be sprinting into the lion's den. If I were to raise that white flag, it would be an indictment against my own convictions. Again, I ignored my gut, walked back inside the house, and asked what time we were getting on the road.

The nerves eventually settled. We found our rhythm. The trip was, thankfully, uneventful. No guns in Kansas City or vandalism in Vegas. Eric plotted a slightly different route than we had taken the two previous times, so it was nice to see some unfamiliar sides of the country. We didn't have the luxury of endless days, so we made good progress and stayed focused. I drove almost the entire time. I'd only had the Jeep for about a month, so I was more comfortable taking the new wheel. Eric didn't seem to mind his duties as the copilot. It was a role he was comfortable playing, and taking into account my disastrous sense of direction, it was also probably the smartest decision.

We steered clear of any potential risks and avoided the emotional soft spots of Kansas City and Vegas entirely. There were some long stretches of silence, common when spending so many hours on the road. But it was never uncomfortable, and we took advantage of the space to reflect on all that was ahead and all we'd left behind. We both had no problem getting lost in our heads for a while. Eric and I were life survivors, and we knew how to fight back. We had a bond that was as strong as steel, and it was something we couldn't completely share with anyone else.

As we got closer to the West Coast, nothing but excitement and anticipation for the checkered flag was on my mind. I relinquished all the worries and I was ready for my rebirth. Even with the occasional body aches and head pressure I'd experienced during our trip, I was optimistic and open. This was what I had been waiting to find. Freedom. My victories and my defeats were going to come from my adventures and not from my condition. It was no longer about grappling with internal obstacles. My battles were now external and tangible, and I was ready for combat.

We swung through familiar streets, and a flood of warm memories rushed over me. The sight of every landmark and storefront from my time in Burbank to my nights in Hollywood brought on a surge of recollection. I was transported physically and emotionally. I tried to pull all the images into my brain, but I quickly realized there was no need. I was back, without deadlines and without time restrictions. I didn't have to soak in every second like a snapshot. This was going to be home. I may not have escaped without scars, but I did escape. The scars were just reminders of all it took to get to that moment.

Eric directed me past the Sunset Strip and up a small semi-private road in the lower Hollywood Hills. They had found a two-bedroom house that they converted for the four of them. That included turning a den and a garage into bedrooms. The plan was for me to crash in a space they called "the nook," which overlooked the kitchen and was adjacent to Eric's bedroom in this open floor plan. I could only imagine what was in store. Everything I knew was about to change. Tim, Stuart, and Matt waited inside. I pulled the Jeep into the driveway and shut off the engine. Eric turned to me with a sly, knowing smile and said, "Let's go say hello."

END

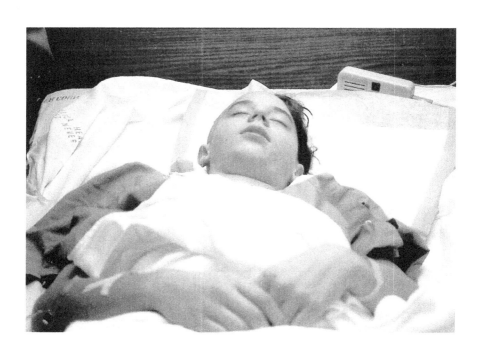